JoAnn
ScrapEssentials™

Idea Book

for Scrapbooking and Paper Crafts

Featuring over **300** new ideas, projects & pages

NANC
& CO.

acknowledgments

The JoAnn ScrapEssential Idea Book for Scrapbooking and Paper Crafts was written by NanC and Company and published by Leisure Arts, Inc.

Author: Nancy M. Hill
Design Director: Candice Snyder
Publications Director: Candice Smoot
Graphic Artist: Rafael Nielson
Cover Design: Rafael Nielson
In House Designers:

       Erin Madsen

       Heather Bakker

       Vanessa Braswell

For information about sales visit the Leisure Arts web site at www.leisurearts.com.

author's letter

Let's face it--
sometimes scrapbookers and paper crafters need fresh ideas!

In the above photo, I am sitting next to a bronze statue created by Dennis Smith. I love this statue because it reminds me of why I scrapbook. It is the same reason most scrapbookers do: to organize and preserve my family's memories and to leave a legacy for those who come after me. I would be delighted if my children and grandchildren cherish the scrapbooks I am making and gathering for them as much as the girl in this statue appears to cherish her book.

We at NanC and Company have been very excited about *The JoAnn ScrapEssential Idea Book for Scrapbooking and Paper Crafts*. Our designers have continued to amaze us with their incredible talent and creativity. Some of their finished projects were so clever we were doing jumping jacks! As always, it is an honor to work with Leisure Arts and JoAnn's and their great team of vendors in this collaborative effort. The JoAnn Essentials products were fun and easy to work with and added an incredible depth to the individual designs and entire project.

This book has been written and designed to assist you with your scrapbooking and paper crafting projects. Whether you are a beginner or seasoned scrapbooker, card maker or paper crafter this book is full of ideas and tips for making great pages and projects. Since most of us have far more photographs than ideas for pages, gifts and projects, we, occasionally, need a "creative boost" and infusion of fresh ideas. We hope the ideas in this book will give you that boost and excite you to create new pages and projects.

Enjoy,

Nancy

Nancy M. Hill of NanC and Company
Founder/President of DieCuts With a View

table of contents

GETTING ORGANIZED

tools to help you get organized

The following tools are handy to have when you are organizing. It is always a good idea to label what you've organized and trim folders and labels to just the right size.

- Scissors
- Label maker
- Address labels
- Permanent marker

organizing photos

Organizing photos is not an easy task with traditional or digital photos, but having them organized allows you to enjoy your photos more and makes them easier to use for scrapbooking and around the house. Getting started can seem overwhelming, so we hope these ideas will ease that feeling and help motivate you to organize your photos.

TRADITIONAL PHOTOS

1. Choose an organizing system.
   a. Choose to organize your photos by date, event, person or however seems appropriate for your collection of photos.
   b. Choose whether you would like to separate photos to scrap, frame and those you would like to keep for sentimental reasons or if you would like to keep all photos together.

2. Choose a storage system.
   a. You can choose the same storage system for all of your photos or choose different storage systems for different purposes. For example, you might choose a bill organizer to hold the photos you want to scrapbook, a small flip album for photos you want to use around the house and a traditional photo album for photos you want to keep, but do not plan on using.
   b. Photo boxes, plastic organizers and photo albums are all good choices for storing photos safely.

1. Choose an organizing system.

   a. Follow the same process of choosing an organizing system as for traditional photos.

2. Choose a storage system.

   a. Choose how you would like to store your photos. You can store them on your hard drive, an external hard drive, Zip discs, CDs, DVDs, online storage services, etc. Even if you choose to keep your photos on your hard drive it is always a good idea to have a backup of your photos.

      i. CDs usually have about 700 megabytes of storage space. The number of photos that can be stored on a CD differ greatly based on the size and quality of your photos.

      ii. DVDs usually have about 4.7 gigabytes of storage space (about seven times the amount of storage space as a CD).

   b. Create folders in which to store your photos. For example, if you organize your photos by event and then by date, you will first choose your "Christmas" folder and then your "2004" folder to see all of your photos from Christmas 2004.

3. Print or develop photos.

   a. Print or develop photos you would like to use on scrapbook pages or in your home. Store these photos the same way you have stored your traditional photos.

ALL PHOTOS

1. Rid yourself of extra photos.

   a. Throw away or delete bad photos you will never use, whether they are blurry, too dark or light, not attractive, or simply bad pictures.

   b. Give away duplicate photos to someone else who will enjoy the photo.

Don't get discouraged by the mass of photos you have to organize. Decide how you would like to organize and store your photos and start following that system with all of your new photos. Then work on your older photos little by little until your organizing system is complete. You can also set aside a large amount of time and organize all of your photos at once.

organizing paper and cardstock

Paper and cardstock are the base for almost every scrapbooking and paper crafting project. Having just the right hue, shade, pattern and scale sets the tone for the entire project. Because of this, we stock up on paper and cardstock so the creative process isn't interrupted by a trip to the store for just the right paper. Now that we have the right paper, the problem is organizing and storing it so we can find it easily in our collection.

PAPER AND CARDSTOCK

1. Choose an organizing system.
   a. Decide how you would like to organize your cardstock. Many people find organizing cardstock by color to be useful. You can follow ROY G BIV (red, orange, yellow, green, blue, indigo, violet) and organize by shade from lightest to darkest. If you like you can keep textured cardstock separate from non-textured cardstock.
   b. Decide how to organize your paper. Choosing a method of organization for paper is a little more complicated than for cardstock. You can organize by color (or main color if it has multiple colors), theme (Halloween, florals) or brand of paper (Memories in the Making, DCWV). Many paper companies have lines that coordinate, so it is nice to keep these papers together. When organizing by theme or brand you can still organize by color within those categories.
   c. You can choose to keep different size paper and cardstock (12 x 12, 8 ½ x 11, 8 x 8, 6 x 6, 5 x 7, 4 x 4) separate from each other or all together.
   d. If you purchase paper and cardstock pads, choose whether to keep the pads separate from the other papers or to tear the pads apart and organize the paper with your loose-leaf paper.

2. Choose a storage system.
   a. There are many different storage options for paper and cardstock. Be sure to choose a storage system that will grow with you, so you don't have to invent a whole new system as your collection grows. Scrappers have had success with the following storage systems: filing cabinets, stacking paper trays, bankers boxes, pizza boxes, purchased paper organizers, accordion files and other products that can be purchased at office supply stores. If you use 12 x 12 paper, make sure that your organizer is at least 12 inches wide.
   b. Create an inventory sheet to place in the front of your organizer or make your own swatch book that can be flipped through quickly to find the perfect paper.

Keep track of paper and cardstock you run out of that you would like to replace so you will know what to buy the next time you go to the store.

organizing scrap paper and cardstock

Your scrap pieces of paper and cardstock can really come in handy. Many scrappers and crafters use different pieces of paper or cardstock on a layout instead of just one full sheet of paper. Don't throw away your scraps; organize them so they can be used again.

1. Choose an organizing system.
   a. Follow the same organizing system you used for your cardstock and patterned paper or keep things simple by keeping both cardstock and paper organized by color in the same place.
2. Choose a storage system.
   a. Page protectors, accordion files, large plastic bags and a file cabinet all work nicely to store your scraps. Make sure your system is large enough to store large scraps, so you won't have to trim them to fit in your storage.

Don't keep scraps that are too small. Keep a recycling bin at your workstation and recycle your scraps that are too small.

organizing stickers

Stickers can tie a page together and create wonderful cards without much effort, but since they come in many different sizes they can be a challenge to organize.

STICKERS

1. Choose an organizing system.
   a. Decide how you would like to keep your stickers organized, whether by theme (School, Birthday, etc.), style (shabby chic, vintage, etc.) or type (cardstock, vellum, etc.) of sticker.
2. Choose a storage system.
   a. Choose a storage system to accommodate the different sized stickers you have. Some ideas are: accordion files, baseball card holders, coupon holders, plastic bags, a tackle box, plastic bin or other purchased organizers.
   b. To make your own baseball card holder to fit different sizes of stickers, sew pockets into a page protector and cut the tops of the pockets open with scissors.

organizing small embellishments

What would we do without embellishments? Can you imagine scrapbooking and paper crafting without eyelets, brads or metal letters? These small embellishments are wonderful additions to our pages and projects, but can be a challenge to organize.

SMALL EMBELLISHMENTS

1. Choose an organizing system.
   a. Most scrappers like to keep each type, color and style of embellishment separate. For example, you might want to have all of your eyelets together, but divided by color and style.
2. Choose a storage system.
   a. It is nice to have a storage system that you can see through so you will not need to label or open the container to see what embellishment is inside. The following containers have worked well for different scrappers: a revolving spice rack, baby food jars, clear film canisters, medicine bottles, tackle boxes, embroidery floss containers and other purchased containers that have individual compartments.
   b. Try to find a storage system that can be opened easily so small embellishments don't go flying out after opening a container.

organizing die cuts

Die cuts help pages come together quickly and easily. With many different shapes and sizes, they too, can pose an organizational dilemma.

DIE CUTS

1. Choose an organizing system.
   a. Choose how to organize your die cuts by theme, size or color.
2. Choose a storage system.
   a. Store die cuts the same way as you have chosen to store your stickers.

organizing fiber, floss and ribbon

Fiber, floss and ribbon add life and texture to a scrapbook page or project. Many scrapbookers have a collection that consists of different sizes, textures and colors that they don't want to become a tangled mess. Hopefully, these ideas will keep your fibers straight.

FIBER, FLOSS AND RIBBON

1. Choose an organizing system.
   a. Choose to organize your fibers by color, type or size.
2. Choose a storage system.
   a. There are many different ways to store fiber, so choose one that works best for you:
      i. Paper towel or toilet paper rolls: wrap many different fibers around each roll and hold in place with tape.
      ii. Plastic bags: fill a plastic bag with one type of ribbon or fiber.
      iii. Empty spool of thread: wrap fiber or floss around the empty spool.
      iv. Cardboard: cut cardboard to desired size, wrap fiber around it and cut a slit in the cardboard so the fiber can be held in place.
      v. Film holders: punch a hole in the lid of the canister, fill the holder with a fiber and thread the end of the fiber through the hole in the lid. Pull out as much thread as you need and trim.

Remember to make sure that your photo storage containers, scrapbooks, sleeves and supplies are all archival safe. Archival safe items will protect your scrapbook pages and photos from degrading over time. Archival safe products are made from acid free, lignin free and PVC/acrylic free materials. Most scrapbooking products will list if they are archival safe on the label so be aware to protect your memories.

There are many more ways to organize your scrapbooking supplies. Be creative and innovative with the items you have at home and be sure to customize your system to fit your needs and your scrapbooking and paper crafting style.

working with

1 cardstock

If there has been one constant in scrapbooking since the beginning, it is cardstock. Cardstock is the foundation of almost every scrapbook page and project. It is versatile, easy to use and can create amazing pages and projects on its own. Even though cardstock has been a staple in scrapbooking and paper crafting, it too has evolved over the years. Cardstock is now available in an array of textures, colors and weights. As new techniques are developed, cardstock changes to meet those needs. From double-sided cardstock for folding and cardstock with a white core for tearing, the following pages will inspire you to use cardstock in new and creative ways.

so stinkin' adorable

Designer: Stacey Stamitoles

Cut strips of patterned paper and adhere to a sheet of cardstock for the background. Adhere a photo to the background and handwrite journaling below the photo. Finish the layout with ribbon, stickers and ink.

ScrapEssentials Jo-Ann

surfin' fun 'n games

Designer: Brenda Nakandakari

Create the background from an assortment of blue cardstock. Paint a strip of transparency with blue paint and adhere below the large photo. Print journaling onto cardstock and the title onto a transparency. Adhere photos to the background and embellish the layout with tiles.

Color can make or break the look of a page faster than anything else. Before you even have time to focus on a photo or title, your mind has already read the colors of a page. Understanding some color basics can really help transform your scrapbook pages into works of art.

The Color Wheel

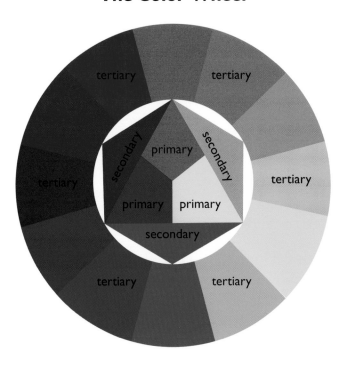

The color wheel is a valuable tool for understanding color, not only does it show the relationship between colors, but it also aids in understanding the following:

- **Complimentary:** A color scheme based on colors opposite each other on the color wheel. These colors balance and contrast each other, enhancing both colors, making them appear more vibrant.
- **Analogous:** A color scheme based on colors adjacent to each other on the color wheel. These colors work well together because they share the same undertones.
- **Monochromatic:** A color scheme based on one color. The color variation comes from different saturations and values of that one color.
- **Hue:** Hue and color are equivalent. Red, yellow and blue are primary colors. Orange, green and purple are secondary colors. Tertiary colors are a combination of two secondary colors.
- **Saturation:** The intensity of color. A fully saturated color is considered to be pure; a less saturated, or grayer, color is muted.
- **Value:** The darkness of color. Light colors are referred to as tints, mid-value colors as midtones, and dark colors as shades.
- **Temperature:** The warmth or coolness of color. Red, orange and yellow are warm colors recalling fire and the sun. Green, blue and purple are cool colors recalling water and grass.

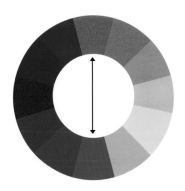

Complimentary

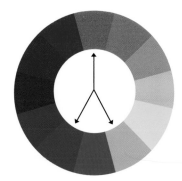

Analogous

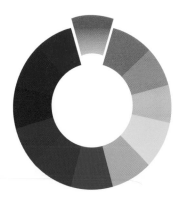

Monochromatic

cardstock

2nd birthday

Designer: Melissa Reynolds

Tear and ink strips of cardstock to create the background. Adhere an inked photo over the strips of cardstock. Embellish the layout with rub-ons, stamps, ink, ribbon, staples and a number stencil.

tearing

Tearing paper and cardstock is one of the fastest and easiest ways to add interest and dimension to projects. Once the cardstock has been torn, it can be left alone, inked, chalked, curled or embossed to add yet another dimension.

Ideas for tearing:

- Wet the area to be torn with a brush, cotton swab or finger. The paper will easily tear along the dampened area
- Tear with the aid of a ruler for a straight tear. Rulers with small and large jagged edges can be purchased to help get the perfect jagged tear
- The straight edge of a table can also aid with a straight tear
- Some cardstock has a white core which gives a nice effect when torn

perfection

Designer: Susan Weinroth

Burn the edges of a sheet of cardstock by carefully lighting small sections of the cardstock on fire. Adhere patterned paper and a photo to the background. Stamp journaling onto a tag and create the title from letter stickers. Embellish the layout with ribbon, photo turns and brads.

pumpkin patch

Designer: Tracy A. Weinzapfel Burgos

Burn names into a rounded stick with a wood burner. Print journaling onto cardstock and tear patterned paper and cardstock for the background. Adhere photos to the background and finish the layout with stickers, stamps, brads and a bottle cap.

cardstock

our little boy lincoln

Designer: NanC & Company Design

Handwrite "B," "O" and "Y" onto cardstock, trim, fit behind silver conchos and cover with clear bubbles. Create the background from cardstock and mat photos with patterned paper. Finish the title with handwriting and rub-ons. Embellish the layout with metal frames, floss, decorative pen markings and a button.

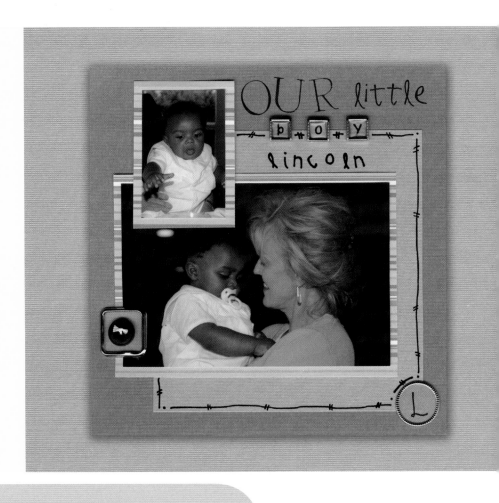

last taste of summer

Designer: Ginger McSwain

Print the title and journaling onto cardstock. Create strips of color by layering strips of cardstock for the background. Adhere photos to the background and embellish the layout with brads, fiber, a vellum tag and 3-D embellishments.

our song

Designer: Tracy A. Weinzapfel Burgos

Print journaling onto a sheet of
cardstock and cut a curve out
of the cardstock. Create the
background from patterned paper,
a large photo and photo corners.
Finish the layout with alphabet
letters, stamps and brads.

megan at 8

Designer: Kelli Dickinson

ScrapEssentials

Trim photos to 4-inch squares and adhere toward the top of a sheet of black cardstock. Adhere strips of paper
above and below the photos and embellish the layout with stamps, rub-ons, metal embellishments and flowers.

cardstock

puppy love

Designer: Cynthia Baula

Print the title onto cardstock and create the background from cardstock and photos. Embellish the layout with handwriting, brads, ribbon, a bookplate and letter stencil.

miracle

Designer: Natalie Quandt

Trim a piece of paper just larger than a photo. Temporarily adhere the paper to the center of a sheet of cardstock and paint around the edges with paint. Remove the paper and adhere the photo inside the painted frame. Create the title with rub-ons and embellish the layout with a flower and brad.

boys and their toys

Designer: Amy L. Barrett-Arthur

Cut cardstock on a curve
and adhere to patterned
paper for the background.
Print title and journaling
onto cardstock, trim and
adhere to the background.
Finish the layout with a
matted photo, ink, stamps,
ribbon, buttons and metal
embellishments.

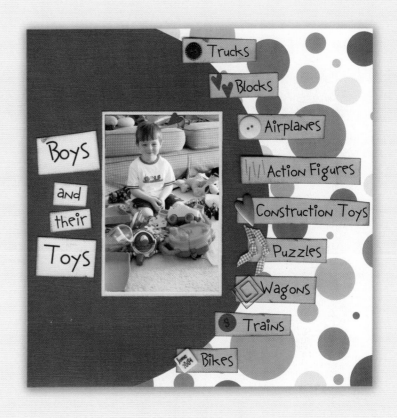

holiday card & tag

Designer: Gayle Hodgins

Card

Create the background by stitching strips
of patterned paper and ribbon to the card.
Embellish the layout with an image, metal phrase,
rub-ons and ink.

Tag

Transfer an image to clear packing tape by printing
the image with a laser printer, rubbing tape over
the image and soaking the tape in water. Rub the
paper off the tape so only the image is left on
the tape and attach the tape to the tag. Stitch
torn patterned paper and ribbon to the tag and
embellish with a metal phrase, ribbon and ink.

cardstock

Step 1

Cut and tear strips of patterned paper and cardstock and adhere to the background overlapping a large photo.

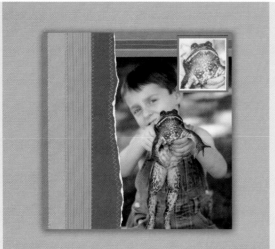

Step 2

Decoratively stitch the cardstock and patterned paper with straight and zigzag stitches. Sand a close-up image, mat with cardstock and adhere to the background.

jackson

Designer: NanC & Company Design

Step 3

Adhere metal letters, tiles, bubbles, a metal bookplate and brads for the name. Finish the layout by threading ribbon and fiber through punched holes.

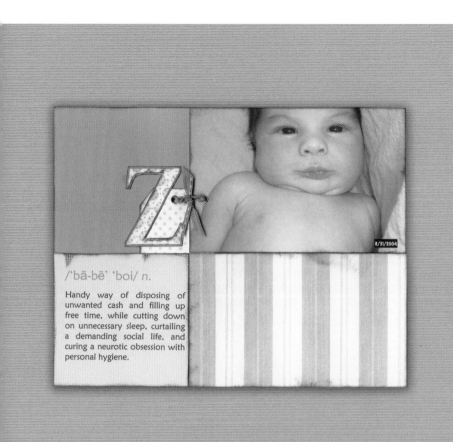

babe boi

Designer: Erica Hernandez

Using a template, cut the letter "Z" out of patterned paper and then cardstock. Print journaling onto cardstock and color block the background. Ink the paper, tag and photo and embellish the layout with ribbon.

if only

Designer: Annette Pixley

Create the background from strips of cardstock and patterned paper. Adhere die cuts, rub-ons, stickers and a matted photo to the background and finish the layout with flower embellishments, brads and handwriting.

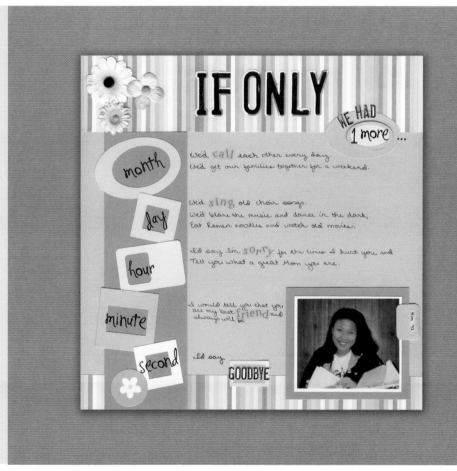

BEING DEEPLY
loved by someone
GIVES YOU STRENGTH;
loving someone deeply
GIVES YOU COURAGE.
Lao-tzu

What a grand thing,
to be loved!
What a grander thing still,
to love!

-Victor Hugo

*a sparkle
in your eyes*

working with
2 vellum &
transparencies

Are you looking for a way to add words and images to your pages without covering up all of your hard work? If so, transparencies and vellum are your answer. These transparent and semi-transparent papers are perfect for titles, journaling, quotes, photos and images. They can be placed directly over photos, patterned paper or an entire layout. Alter your vellum and transparencies with paint, chalk and ink or use them for image transfers and photo manipulation. However you choose to use them, you will enjoy their versatility.

cheerfulness

Designer: Rachael Giallongo

Attach a vellum quote over patterned paper to the background with staples. Adhere a photo to the background and stickers for the title. Embellish the layout with staples, ribbon, ink and labels.

fieldtrip

Designer: Heather Uppencamp

Print title and journaling onto a transparency and place over mesh and a photo. Print the rest of the journaling onto canvas and trim. Mat photos and adhere to the background. Finish the layout with canvas numbers and metal embellishments.

Step 1

Trim a piece of cardstock to fit into a plastic photo flip album. Adhere torn cardstock to the background.

Step 2

Mat a photo with cardstock and ink the mat with brown ink. Ink a vellum quote with brown ink and adhere over the photo.

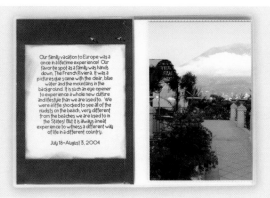

european vacation

Designer: NanC & Company Design

ScrapEssentials JoAnn

Step 3

Adhere another inked vellum quote over the photo and create the title from letter and number stickers. Ink a metal bookplate with brown ink and attach over the number stickers with black brads. Slide the layout into the front of the plastic photo flip album.

flowers heal the soul

Designer: Sherry Wright

Print the title and journaling onto a transparency and highlight the text by painting behind the text. Create the background from torn and inked patterned paper. Mat the photos and ink the mats. Finish the layout with lace, ribbon and a ribbon charm.

kale & mums

Designer: Sam Cousins

Cut out letters from vellum for the title and attach letter stickers over the vellum title. Create the background from patterned paper and photos. Mat two photos and ink the paper. Attach a transparency quote over the small photo and finish the layout with ribbon.

waikiki beach

Designer: Katie Watson

Print journaling onto vellum and tear and ink the edges. Create the background from torn and inked patterned paper and cardstock. Embellish the layout with a photo, postcard, quote, raffia, bookplate, brads, photo corners and handwriting.

photo manipulation

Manipulating photos has become something that even the novice photographer can do thanks to software programs such as Photoshop. Software programs allow you to manipulate digital images (either taken with a digital camera, or a hard copy scanned) with ease. Manipulation of photos can also be done manually with hard copy photos. Experiment with manipulating your photos to add variety and interest to your pages and projects.

Ideas for photo manipulation:

- Change photos from color to black and white or sepia tone
- Add color to a key element in a black and white photo
- Experiment with the different filters on your software program (these can make your photo look like a cartoon, painting, sketch or blurry, etc.)
- Crop your image in different ways
- Sand the edges of a photo or the entire photo
- Cover a photo with vellum
- Tear, ink and paint the edges of a photo

- Cut a photo into pieces and adhere to a sheet of paper with spaces in-between the cuts like a mosaic
- Cut portions of a double print and adhere to the original with pop dots
- Print photos onto fabric, cardstock, vellum or transparencies
- Transfer images using tape or other methods
- Put color, black and white and sepia tone photos on the same page or project
- Reverse print an image on the wrong side of a transparency to create a rub-on

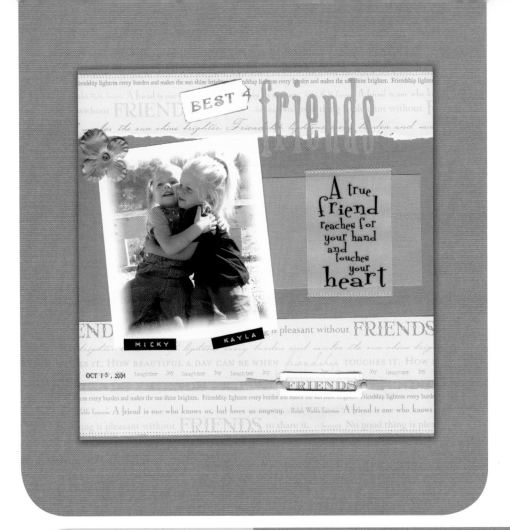

best friends

Designer: Tracy A. Weinzapfel Burgos

Paint metal embellishments and create the background from torn and cut patterned paper and cardstock. Zigzag stitch paper and a vellum quote to the background. Adhere the photo to the background and embellish the layout with ribbon, brads, labels, stamps, floss, a flower and button.

ScrapEssentials Jo-Ann

limbo, limbo, limbo!

Designer: Melissa Smith

Print the title and journaling onto a transparency. Create the background from patterned paper and a curved photo. Embellish the layout with stamps, 3-D embellishments and raffia.

kiss

Designer: Mary Jo Johnston

Color block the background with patterned paper. Mat photos and a vellum quote and adhere to the background. Adhere a printed vellum strip and a patterned paper strip below the photos. Embellish the layout with metals, brads, ribbon, a page pebble and word pebble.

my time

Designer: Tracy A. Weinzapfel Burgos

Zigzag stitch patterned paper and a transparency to the background. Print journaling onto cardstock and vellum and mat and ink the journaling. Finish the layout with stickers, stamps, ribbon and a ribbon charm.

Scrap**Essentials** Jo·Ann

meant to be

Designer: Sara Bryans

Print journaling onto cardstock, mat, ink and adhere to the background. Hand stitch a transparency over the background. Attach a photo over the journaling and transparency with metal hinges. Embellish the layout with metals.

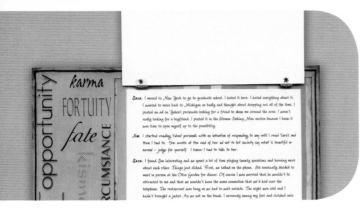

chalk

Ideas for chalking:

- Emphasize a word by highlighting it with chalk
- Mix different colors of chalk before applying to the page or blend colors together after they have been applied to the page
- Chalk the edges of a photo
- Chalk the background of a page

Chalking is an easy way to add color to a project. Chalk comes in a variety of colors and can easily be applied to almost any surface. Apply chalk to a page with cotton swabs, tissue, a finger or sponge. Use reverse-action handle tweezers to hold a cotton swab to make the application even easier. Simply rub a cotton swab over the chalk and apply to the project. If you would like a lighter application, dab the cotton swab onto a paper towel before applying the chalk to your page.

live in the moment

Designer: NanC & Company Design

Sand metal tags with sandpaper, stamp with letter stamps, thread ribbon through the holes of the tags and attach to the page with brads. Adhere photos, patterned paper and a chalked vellum quote to the background.

tennis

Designer: NanC & Company Design

Print journaling onto vellum and adhere over the right side of the page. Create the background from patterned paper and cardstock. Mat photos and ink the mats. Embellish the layout with ribbon, metal letters, metal words and brads.

sisters

Designer: Keisha Campbell

Round the corners of a transparency and adhere over inked patterned paper. Adhere a photo to the background leaving space for a tag to slide behind the photo. Create a tag from cardstock and embellish the layout with ribbon, brads, tacks, painted metals, stickers and a letter stencil.

our family

Designer: NanC & Company Design

Tear a vellum quote and adhere to the background surrounding a photo. Create the background from patterned paper. Mat a photo and embellish the layout with buttons, brads, vellum, metal tags and fiber.

little woolen stockings

Designer: Katie Watson

Tear a quote, ink the edges and adhere over a photo and patterned paper. Create the background from torn, sanded and inked patterned paper. Tear and ink the edges of a photo and embellish the layout with letter stickers, ribbon, brads, stamps, handwriting, a bookplate, button and charm.

me

Designer: Sandi Minchuk

Create the background from distressed patterned papers and a photo. Adhere a transparency to the background and embellish the layout with photo turns, photo corners, a tape measure and a heat embossed metal-rimmed tag and metal letters.

bliss

I

love

scrapbooking

sweet

wish

friend

working with

3 # patterned paper

Do you remember when patterned paper was used solely as a background for scrapbook pages? Now patterned paper has boundless uses only limited by your imagination. In this section you will see patterned paper used to create gift bags, baby mobiles, collage backgrounds and interesting embellishments. You will see paper torn, inked, crumpled and cut into shapes. With one piece of paper you can add interest, color, dimension and pattern to your pages. Try using this great mainstay in a way you never have before on your next layout or project.

colorful you

Designer: Heather Thompson

Create the background from patterned paper and a photo. Cut quotes from patterned paper and adhere to the page. Finish the layout with leather flowers, ribbon, acrylic squares, brads and a chipboard letter.

water lily

Designer: Erika Hayes

Round the corners and ink the edges of strips of patterned paper to create the background. Mat a photo, ink the mat and adhere to the background. Embellish the layout with inked quotes, letter stickers, handwritten journaling, ribbon, flowers and a paper clip.

sour

Designer: Brandy Brandon

Create the background
by adhering rectangles of
patterned paper to cardstock.
Adhere photos to the
background and journaling
printed onto vellum. Embellish
the layout with letter stickers,
brads and a metal bookplate.

ScrapEssentials JoAnn

love bag

Designer: Leah Fung

Create a gift bag from folded
and stitched patterned paper.
Mat a 3-D embellishment with
patterned paper and cardstock
and embellish the layout with
ribbon, stitching and eyelets.

patterned paper

happy family

Designer: Krista Fernandez

Create the background from torn patterned paper and cardstock. Mat and adhere a photo to the background. Handwrite journaling onto cardstock and finish the layout with metal embellishments, flowers, ribbon and letter stickers.

happy birthday tag

Designer: Anna Estrada Davison

Create a tag from patterned paper and ink the edges. Punch square holes and tie ribbon through the holes. Embellish the tag with stickers, brads, metal letters, a bookplate and 3-D embellishment.

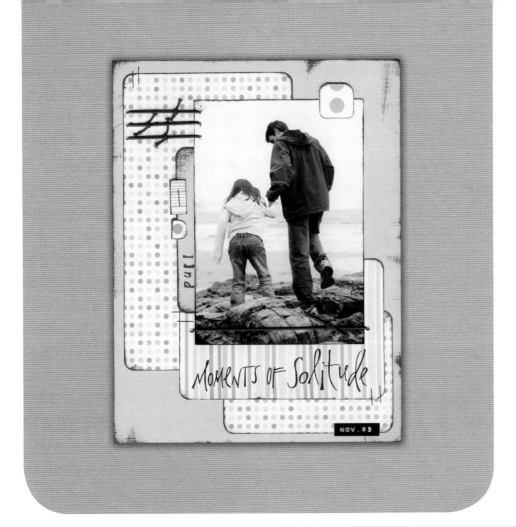

moments
of solitude

Designer: Melissa Reynolds

Adhere inked patterned paper onto cardstock for the background. Adhere an inked photo to the background leaving space for a tag to slide behind the photo. Punch holes into the background, thread with elastic and tie into knots. Embellish the layout with rub-ons, staples and a label.

who are you?

Designer: Sam Cousins

Cut circles of patterned paper and adhere to the background. Print journaling onto patterned paper and adhere photos to the background. Embellish the layout with ribbon, ink, brads, a tag and metal word.

patterned paper

the ups & downs of anna grace

Designer: Felicia Krelwitz

Create the background from torn, inked and sanded patterned paper. Adhere a matted photo to the background leaving space for a tag to slide behind the photo. Mat a photo and tear and ink the mat to create a tag. Embellish the layout with letter stickers, stamps, handwriting, ribbon, metal brads and a quote.

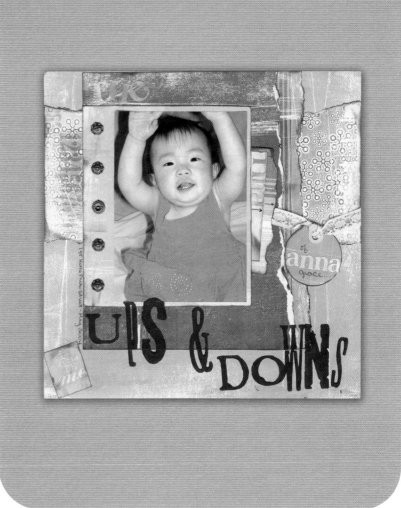

just a little note

Designer: Colorbok, Inc.

Tin

Stamp the title onto cardstock and adhere to a tin behind a metal frame. Wrap a ribbon around the tin and tie into a bow.

Cards

Create cards from folded patterned paper. Stitch cardstock onto the cards and finish with metal embellishments, ribbon, stamps and bubbles.

chatty girl

Designer: Elizabeth Cuzzacrea

Create the background from patterned paper, photos and a tag. Create the title from stamps and letter stickers. Embellish the layout with labels, staples, brads, metal embellishments, ribbon, a card and tag.

vacation mode

Designer: Susan Weinroth

Stitch fabric to cardstock and patterned paper to fabric to create the background. Mat a photo and print journaling onto cardstock. Embellish the layout with letter stencils, rubons, stamps, ribbon, flowers and metal embellishments.

loved

Designer: Keisha Campbell

Ink the edges and round the
corners of patterned paper to
create the background. Mat a
photo, ink a tag and quote and
slide the tag behind the photo.
Embellish the layout with a
strip of transparency, pearl
ribbon slide, metal-rimmed tag,
flower, letter stickers, ribbon,
cardstock tags, tacks and brads.

it's about time

Designer: Jennifer Miller

Create a pocket from strips
of inked patterned paper. Mat
a photo and print journaling
onto cardstock. Embellish the
layout with stickers, stamps,
alphabet charms, ribbon, ink
and a wooden flower.

life is groovy

Designer: Christine Traversa

Adhere strips of cardstock and patterned paper to the background. Adhere a photo at an angle over a mat. Embellish the layout with stickers, ribbon and buttons.

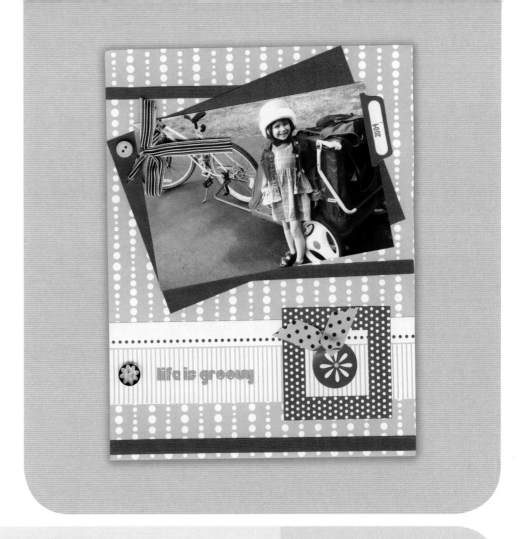

you are mine

Designer: Andrea Mette

Create the background from painted patterned paper, cardstock and a photo. Embellish the layout with ribbon, metal embellishments, letter stickers, a flower and bead.

patterned paper

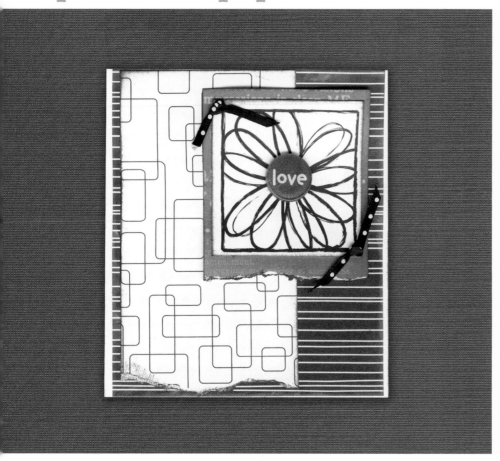

love card
Designer: Erin R. Wells

Tear and ink patterned paper, adhere to the card and embellish with ribbon and an acrylic word.

Scrap Essentials™ Jo-Ann

don't bug me
Designer: Ginger McSwain

Create the background from inked patterned paper and cardstock. Adhere photos to the background and create the title from letter die cuts. Embellish the layout with 3-D embellishments, labels and handwritten and printed journaling.

happy holidays card

Designer: Jlyne Hanback

Adhere patterned paper behind the openings of an overlay and adhere the overlay to a card. Embellish the card with metal embellishments and ribbon.

merry christmas card

Designer: Bea Elizalde

Double mat patterned paper with cardstock and embellish the card with ribbon.

patterned paper

eloquent kiss

Designer: Brandi Olsovsky

Create a stained glass effect
with patterned paper and black
cardstock. Frame a photo with
metal embellishments and
cardstock. Finish the layout
with a handwritten tag and
embellish the tag with rub-ons,
ribbon and a paper clip.

color blocking

Color blocking is an excellent way to create a background for a page. Color blocking is simply creating blocks of color on
a page. The blocks can be made from cardstock, paper and vellum or they can be made digitally. They can be symmetrical
or asymmetrical, squares, rectangles, circles or stripes. Color blocking can be bold with bright colors or subtle with a
monochromatic theme. This technique can create visually pleasing, clean and simple pages.

Ideas for color blocking:

- Make blocks from bright colored cardstock
- Use fabric instead of a paper product to create your
  blocks
- Use patterned paper instead of just solid colors
- Create strips of color from ribbon

hi card

Designer: Miranda Isenberg

Embellish a canning lid with paint, patterned paper, mesh, ribbon, metal embellishments and tiles with rub-on letters. Create the background from patterned paper, cardstock and ribbon wrapped around the card.

quinn

Designer: Tarri Botwinski

Create the background from strips of patterned paper and twill tape. Punch out the vellum of metal rimmed tags and emboss with Ultra Thick Embossing Enamel (UTEE). Print journaling onto cardstock, trim, ink and stitch to the background. Embellish the layout with letter stickers, metal phrases and brads.

patterned paper

Step 1

Cut a square of cardstock and patterned paper and adhere with the wrong sides together. Cut four slits from the corners of the square and create a pinwheel by adhering one folded side of each triangle to the center of the square.

Step 2

Stitch a button to the center of each pinwheel.

baby mobile

Designer: NanC & Company Design

Step 3

Adhere each pinwheel to a piece of ribbon. Tie the other side of the ribbon to a quilting hoop with a bow. Attach the quilting hoop to the ceiling with ribbon.

happy
Designer: Kathy Bishop

Fold the corners of patterned
paper and glue a contrasting
patterned paper to the fold. Tack
the folds down with brads. Create
the background from inked pieces
of patterned paper. Mat a photo
and embellish the layout with
photo turns, brads, rub-ons, ribbon
and a metal-rimmed tag.

Scrap Essentials Jo-Ann

experience rome
Designer: NanC & Company Design

Ink cardstock and patterned paper
with ink. Mat a photo and metal
letters and ink the mats with ink.
Accent the page with fiber, metal
embellishments, letter and date
stamps and page pebbles.

Scrap Essentials Jo-Ann

blue eyed beauty

Designer: Sandra Liddell

Print journaling onto patterned paper, tear and ink. Cut out the title from patterned paper and embellish the layout with eyelets, fiber, ink and patterned paper.

Scrap Essentials Jo-Ann

smile

Designer: Jen Ussai

Create the background from strips of inked patterned paper and cardstock. Mat a photo and embellish the layout with metal letters, gems, ribbon, letter stamps and a cardstock tag.

crumpling

Crumpling paper is one of the easiest ways to add interest and texture to your pages. Simply wad the paper into a ball and then flatten for use on your page. Try crumpling paper, cardstock, stickers and vellum.

Ideas for crumpling:

- Dampen the paper with walnut ink and water before crumpling
- Modge podge crumpled paper
- After crumpling, ink the edges of paper
- After crumpling, ink the entire sheet so the high points will catch the ink
- Crumple paper over and over again to get the look and feel of fabric
- Tear crumpled paper
- Iron paper flat after crumpling

friendship

Designer: Susan Stringfellow

Dampen the background paper with water and walnut ink, crumple and ink lightly with an inkpad. Stitch the patterned paper to the card. Sand and ink all other patterned paper and cardstock. Finish the card with an inked quote, walnut inked flowers, tacks and brads.

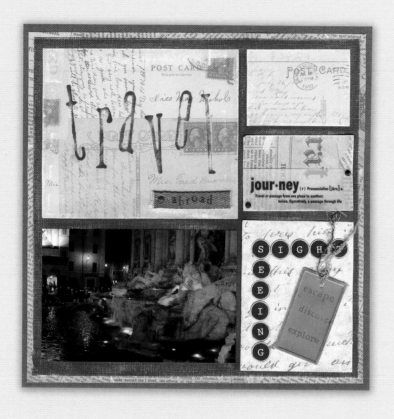

travel abroad
Designer: NanC & Company Design

Create the background from sanded patterned paper and cardstock. Color block the background with patterned paper and a photo. Embellish the layout with letter stickers, stamps, brads, a metal-rimmed tag, quote and 3-D embellishment.

brothers
Designer: Kerry Umbanhowar

Cut a large circle from patterned paper, ink the edges and trim what doesn't fit on the page. Mat a photo, ink the mat and adhere to the background leaving space for a tag to slide behind the photo. Embellish the layout with stamps, rub-ons, ribbon, handwriting and a label.

treasure

Designer: Vicki Chrisman

Photographer: Keith Jenkins

Create the background from a collage of inked patterned paper and cardstock. Adhere a photo to the background. Ink a letter stencil, back with cardstock and stitch around the edges. Frame a word with a wooden frame and attach to the page with strips of cardstock and rivets. Finish the layout with handwritten journaling, pieces of patterned paper and a date stamp.

walnut ink

Walnut ink is a great way to get an aged look, quickly! You can use walnut ink on paper, cardstock, vellum, stickers, fabric, wood, cork and more. Simply combine the walnut ink crystals with water and brush the ink onto your medium to get the desired effect. The less water used, the more intense the color will be. Follow the directions on the packaging for how much water in relation to crystals to use.

Ideas for walnut ink:

- Crumple and tear the edges of cardstock before applying walnut ink
- Ink a vellum quote
- Ink paper embellishments
- Ink the background of a photo transfer
- Ink fabric, ribbon and fiber

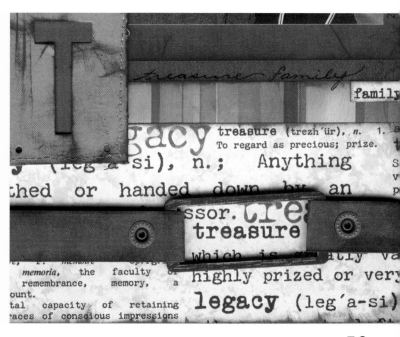

working with
4 brads & eyelets

Brads and eyelets are truly the nuts and bolts of scrapbooking. Their uses are limitless as binders or purely decorative embellishments especially with the variety of colors, shapes and sizes that are available. Many crafters alter brads and eyelets with sandpaper, paint and ink and use these staples in unpredictable ways. Learn unique ways other crafters use brads and eyelets in this chapter to help make your pages even more extraordinary.

brads
& eyelets

savor

Designer: Linda Beeson

Cut strips of patterned paper, round the edges and attach to cardstock with brads for the background. Mat a photo and finish the layout with ribbon, ink and a metal word.

giggle

Designer: Laura Vegas

Attach eyelets to strips of blue cardstock, weave floss through the eyelets and adorn with photos. Create the background from torn cardstock. Embellish the layout with ribbon, definition stickers, chalk and handwriting.

forever card

Designer: Colorbok, Inc.

Create a tag pocket from patterned paper and stitching. Create a card by attaching eyelets to the top of a piece of cardstock. Embellish the card with jump rings, ribbon, patterned paper, stitching and a vellum quote and embellish the pocket with a fabric word, metal bookplate and brads.

eyelet setter

Eyelets are handy scrapbooking supplies that are both functional and decorative. In order to use eyelets, though, one must have an eyelet setter. The good thing is that eyelet setters are quick and easy to use. First, a hole the size of the eyelet needs to be created with a hole punch or eyelet tool. Second, the eyelet is placed in the hole and turned upside down so the back of the eyelet is facing up. Third, an eyelet setter is used to press the back of the eyelet down so that the eyelet has a firm hold on the paper.

There are two kinds of eyelet setters on the market:

1. Hammer setter: This set of tools main components are an eyelet punch, setter and hammer. Simply hammer the tops of the tools like you would a nail to set the eyelet.

2. Spring setter: This set uses the force of a spring to punch a hole and set an eyelet instead of a hammer. Simply lift the top of the spring while holding the base of the spring and let go of the top portion of the spring. The spring will come back down with force to set the eyelet.

Ideas for using an eyelet setter:

- Use a protective mat under the eyelet to protect your table or desk
- Use eyelet setters on a sturdy surface

brads & eyelets

Step 1

Cover the front of a gift bag with patterned paper.

Step 2

Mat transparent stickers with cardstock and attach to the bag with brads, eyelets and ribbon.

congratulations gift bag

Designer: NanC & Company Design

Step 3

Adorn the bag with metal tile brads.

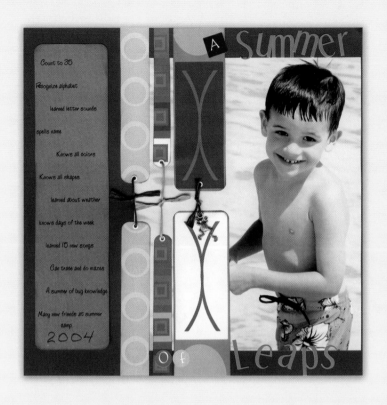

a summer of leaps

Designer: Jackie Siperko

Cut strips of patterned paper,
round the corners and ink the
edges. Attach eyelets to the
patterned paper and thread with
raffia. Create the background from
cardstock and a photo. Embellish
the layout with printed cardstock,
letter stickers and a metal charm.

red, white
& blue

Designer: Tarri Botwinski

Ink metal tags, attach letter
stickers and then heat emboss
with Ultra Thick Embossing
Enamel (UTEE). Create the
background from patterned
paper, cardstock and photos.
Cut out the title from patterned
paper and print journaling
onto cardstock. Embellish the
layout with fabric, star cutouts,
brads, chalk, stitching and a 3-D
embellishment.

brads & eyelets

a trip to remember album

Designer: Cassonda Tadlock

Paint the front of face cards, attach eyelets in each corner and create an album by tying the cards together with flax through the eyelets. Embellish each card as desired.

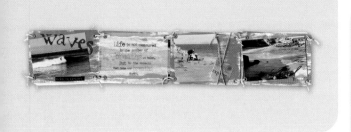

christmas tree tag

Designer: Sam Cousins

Stitch brown and green ribbon to patterned paper and attach brads to the green ribbon. Create a tag from patterned paper and cardstock and embellish the tag with metal embellishments, ribbon and ink.

celebrate good times

Designer: Nannette Coffey

Adhere patterned paper onto a card and attach eyelets to the patterned paper. Create an envelope from vellum and a tag from patterned paper. Embellish the layout with floss, photo turns, stamps, letter stickers, a label and brad.

rebel

Designer: Kim Musgrove

Print journaling onto cardstock and ink the edges. Create the background from patterned paper and photos. Finish the layout with brads, stickers and labels.

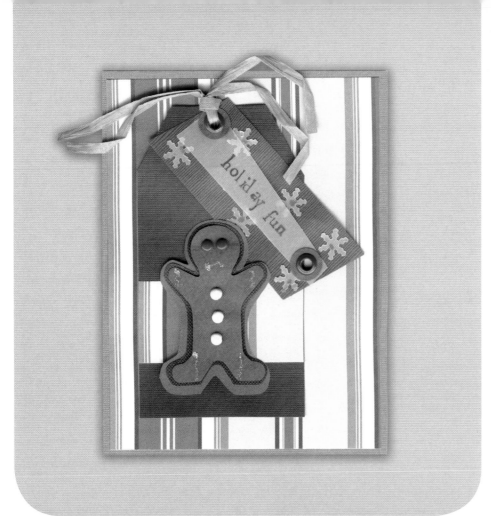

gingerbread boy card

Designer: Bea Elizalde

Create a gingerbread boy from cardstock, brads and glitter. Embellish the card with patterned paper, cardstock, eyelets, stamped and cut vellum and raffia.

gingerbread girl card

Designer: Bea Elizalde

Create a gingerbread girl from cardstock, brads and glitter. Embellish the card with patterned paper and printed vellum.

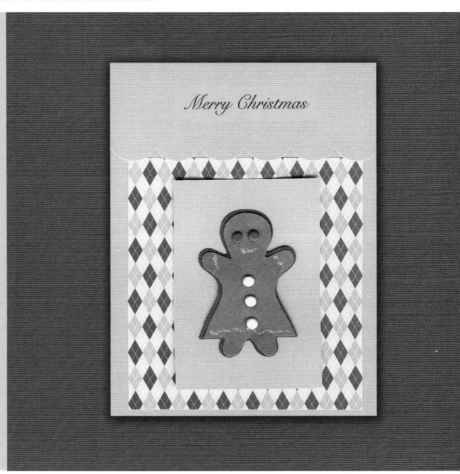

jolly

Designer: Susan Stringfellow

Create a tag from a letter stencil, patterned paper and cardstock. Sand the cardstock, stitch together and finish by attaching fiber to the bottom with brads. Create the background from cardstock, patterned paper and a photo. Embellish the layout with ribbon, metal embellishments, stitching, stamps and a printed transparency.

my favorite things about fall

Designer: Vicki Chrisman

Stamp journaling and part of the title onto paper, trim and attach to the background with brads. Fold and staple a tag to create a pocket. Embellish the layout with ribbon, photos, tags, twill, metal embellishments, stickers and a label.

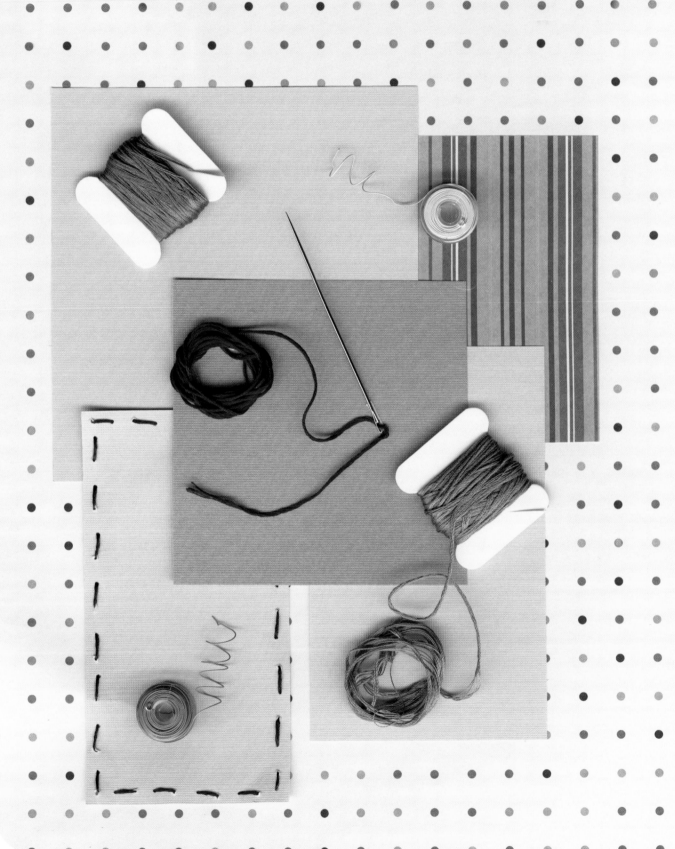

working with

5 floss, wire & thread

If you want to give a page or project a homemade feel, try adding floss, wire and thread as a decorative, yet functional addition to your projects. Floss and thread are great for stitching and threading beads, while wire is great for making into letters and shapes, binding books and threading beads and charms. Make floss, wire and thread part of your paper crafting basics and you will discover their many uses.

silly

Designer: NanC & Company Design

Stitch a collage of patterned paper to cardstock. Print the title onto patterned paper, trim and adhere to the background. Finish the layout with a matted photo, quote and buttons.

learn

Designer: Janet Hopkins

Stitch inked patterned paper to the background. Print the title onto patterned paper and the journaling onto cardstock to slide behind the photo. Embellish the layout with ribbon and painted metals.

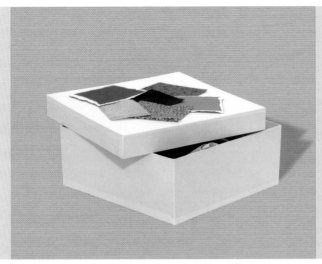

Step 1

Cut and tear irregular squares of fabric and cardstock.

Step 2

Modge podge the fabric and cardstock onto the box.
Wrap fabric around the perimeter of the lid.

Scrap Essentials Jo-Ann

nana's keepsake box

Designer: NanC & Company Design

Step 3

Hand stitch the title and a flower
onto cardstock and adhere to
the top of the box. Finish the box
by wrapping ribbon around the
perimeter of the lid.

family is forever

Designer: Mikki Livanos

Create a tag pocket by folding and stitching cardstock. Cut tags from cardstock and age everything with ink and chalk. Embellish the tag pocket with ribbon, brads, flower and a linen letter.

the perfect day

Designer: Mary Jo Johnston

Create the title and journaling from cardstock, patterned paper, stamps and ribbon. Adhere torn, inked and cut patterned paper and cardstock to the background. Mat and ink photos and embellish the layout with buttons, floss, brads, a flower, safety pin and bookplate.

safe in brothers arms

Designer: Janet Hopkins

Stitch a strip of patterned paper to cardstock. Print the title onto twill tape and the journaling onto a transparency. Mat two photos, ink the mats and outline the photos with paint. Embellish the layout with rub-ons, twill tape, metals and staples.

unconditional love

Designer: Melissa Koehler

Stamp the title onto patterned paper, add red accents with a paintbrush and finish the title with rub-ons. Frame the title with a large bookplate. Create the background from torn and inked patterned paper, cardstock and photos. Embellish the layout with small photos, ribbon, wire, a painted frame and stamp.

floss, wire & thread

just add water
Designer: Sam Cousins

Adhere a torn photo overlapping two larger photos. Finish the layout with rub-ons and pre-strung beaded wire embellishments.

warm wishes card
Designer: Michelle Gowland ScrapEssentials JoAnn

Punch holes 1/8 inch apart from one another around three circles of cardstock. Stitch a pattern around the circles. Stitch the snowflakes and arms and embellish the layout with brads, gemstones and a die cut.

miracle of christmas magnet
Designer: Susan Stringfellow ScrapEssentials JoAnn

Twist a piece of wire to form swirls and wrap it around a pencil or nail to form coils. Adorn the wire with beads and charms as you go. Adhere inked patterned paper to a cardboard coaster for the background and attach a magnet to the back of the coaster. Embellish the magnet with a photo, stamps and metal embellishments.

thankful

Designer: Tarri Botwinski

Draw curved lines from patterned paper leaves and hand stitch along the lines. Hand stitch a vellum quote to cardstock and frame the quote with stitched cardstock and brads. Create the background from patterned paper, cardstock and a matted photo. Create the title from a letter sticker and patterned paper and finish the layout with 3-D embellishments and hand stitching.

snowman card

Designer: Lynda Mekata

Embroider a snowman onto cardstock using an embroidery machine. Put fabric behind the cardstock so the thread won't tear through the cardstock. Attach the embroidered cardstock to a card with brads.

floss, wire & thread

hand stitching

If you want to add charm, texture and a homemade feel to a page, hand stitching is your answer. All you will need is some floss, a needle and thimble (if desired). There is no right or wrong way to stitch, so come up with a stitch on your own or choose from many established stitches including: back stitches, cross stitches, chain stitches, blanket stitches, knotted stitches, satin stitches and more. Feel free to use floss, thread, fiber, jute and even ribbon with your stitching.

Ideas for hand stitching:

- Stitch images on your projects
- Use at least three strands of floss or all six to make the stitching really stand out
- Weave fiber through the background of a page
- Stitch seams of paper
- Stitch the top of a flap or photo to reveal photos or journaling underneath
- Thread ribbon through eyelet holes
- Stitch letters and words

the fruits of our labor

Designer: Heather Uppencamp

Hand stitch a photo to patterned paper. Tear, ink and curl the edge of a piece of patterned paper and adhere over the background. Print journaling onto a transparency, adhere over a photo onto a tag and slide into a vellum envelope. Sand and ink photos and finish the layout with rub-ons, ribbon and string.

forever

Designer: NanC & Company Design

Hand stitch a collage of patterned paper and cardstock for the background. Print journaling onto vellum and finish the journaling with hand stitching. Mat a photo and embellish the layout with rub-ons, ribbon, metal bookplates and a metal charm.

reflections of you

Designer: Lily Goldsmith

Stitch burlap to the background and cover with journaling printed onto a transparency. Mat a photo at an angle and embellish the layout with stickers, rub-ons, brads, handwriting and a monogram letter.

working with
6 fiber, ribbon & fabric

Fiber, ribbon and fabric make a big impact on your pages and projects by adding texture, interest, color and dimension. There are countless ways to use fiber, ribbon and fabric on your projects as shown in this section. Notice ribbon made into a purse, a photo printed onto fabric and fiber used to embellish books.

fiber, ribbon & fabric

escape pocket book

Designer: Me & My Big Ideas

Create a pocket book from sheets of patterned paper folded in half to create pockets and tied together with raffia. Fill each pocket with a tag embellished with photos and raffia.

under the tuscan sun

Designer: Alicia Irby

Create the background from patterned paper and a large photo. Adhere a ribbon to the background separating the photo and paper. Finish the layout with a metal clip, metal-rimmed tag and string.

my little angel

Designer: Monique Mclean

Create a flap to hide journaling by folding a rectangle of cardstock in half and journaling on the inside of the flap. Create the background from patterned paper, cardstock, ribbon and a photo. Embellish the layout with rub-ons, flowers, brads, a bookplate, label and paper clip.

christmas card

Designer: Randi Lanz

Thread a metal charm with twisted fiber. Create the background from patterned paper and inked cardstock and finish the card with stickers, star brads and silver tinsel.

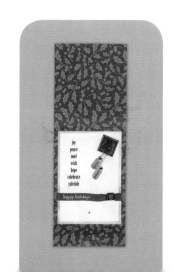

fiber, ribbon & fabric

precious

Designer: Sharon Laakkonen

Print a photo onto aida cloth and fray the edges. Print the title, name and age onto aida cloth and trim. Create the background from torn and inked patterned paper and cardstock. Print journaling onto a transparency and finish the layout with flowers, metal charms, torn photos and ribbon.

sewing machine

Get out your sewing machines again, scrappers! Your neglected sewing machine can help add interest and texture to your pages without much effort or bulk. You don't need to be an expert seamstress to add stitching to your pages and projects, either. Simply take a minute to become familiar with your sewing machine again and you will be ready to go.

- Notice the different stitches of which your sewing machine is capable. Most have a straight and zigzag stitch, but many have a variety of decorative stitches to choose from.
- Make sure to properly thread your machine and bobbin.
- Practice a selected stitch on scratch paper. If the thread isn't pulling equally on both sides, adjust the tension.
- Start sewing on your pages and have fun!

Ideas for sewing:

- Stitch pieces of paper together to create a background
- Zigzag stitch the corners of a photo
- Stitch elements onto tags
- Stitch the border of a photo or entire page

ballet frame

Designer: Jlyne Hanback

Cut a mat from patterned paper, wrap ribbon below the photo and place behind a glass frame. Embellish the frame with 3-D embellishments.

swing

Designer: Tammy Gauck

Tie small pieces of ribbon onto a long piece of ribbon and adhere to the top of the page. Create the background from patterned paper and an inked photo. Print the title and journaling onto a transparency and finish the layout with a tag, label, handwriting and ribbon.

fiber, ribbon & fabric

Step 1

Seal standard envelopes and cut in half to create pockets. Accordion fold patterned paper for the binding and adhere the envelopes to the folds.

Step 2

Create tags from cardstock. Cover the envelopes and tags with torn patterned paper and cardstock.

our little man tag book

Designer: NanC & Company Design

Step 3

Embellish the pockets and tags with photos, fiber and embellishments.

sunshine, freedom and a little flower

Designer: Felicia Krelwitz

Cut strips of fabric, fray the edges and wrap around patterned paper and cardstock. Create the background from patterned paper and cardstock. Embellish the layout with matted photos, a transparency quote, flower, metal charm, tag and handwriting.

dear santa door hanger

Designer: Sam Cousins

Cover a square of corrugated cardboard on both sides with inked patterned paper. Punch two holes toward the top and thread with ribbon. Embellish the squares with matted photos, metal letters, stickers and ribbon.

goofey's kitchen
Designer: Michelle Hubbartt

Weave ribbon in and out of square holes in patterned paper. Create the background from inked patterned paper and a photo. Create the title from stickers and print journaling onto a transparency. Embellish the layout with metal embellishments and ribbon.

love
Designer: Brandy Brandon

Create the background from patterned paper and a photo. Tie ribbon in a knot down the side of the page. Finish the layout with journaling printed onto cardstock, staples, buttons, brads, letters and photo turns.

regan

Designer: Laura Alpuché

Create the background from torn
and inked patterned paper and
cardstock. Mat a photo and ink the
mat. Tie pieces of ribbon around a
strip of cardstock and patterned
paper. Embellish the layout with
rub-ons, a date stamp and
metal phrase.

let it snow card

Designer: Jlyne Hanback

Print the title onto a transparency and adhere
behind the opening of an overlay. Adhere
patterned paper behind the openings of the
overlay and adhere the overlay to a card. Finish the
card with metal embellishments, fiber and ribbon.

35 years

Designer: Cassonda Tadlock

Attach striped ribbon to a card with brads.
Embellish the card with torn patterned paper,
stickers, stamps, string, a vellum tag and a safety pin.

grandma
mini album

Designer: Wendy Malichio

Adhere a chalked vellum quote over dry brushed acrylic paint. Embellish the layout with a bookplate, sticker, 3-D embellishment and ribbon.

collage necklace

Designer: Colorbok, Inc.

Trim a definition and photo to fit inside a metal frame, tape the collage to the back of the frame and modge podge the front. Tie ribbon to the frame and attach with necklace ends.

miah clipboard

Designer: Anna Estrada Davison

Color block the clipboard with patterned paper, modge podge and paint. Drill five holes in the bottom of the clipboard and thread with ribbon. Embellish the clipboard with a matted photo, 3-D embellishment, painted bookplate, stickers, stamps, buttons and ribbon.

sewing purse

Designer: Arlana Patten

Weave ribbon and measuring tape and sew to create a purse. Line the purse with fabric, attach handles and keep the purse closed with measuring tape and a button. Embellish the purse with needles and thread.

fiber, ribbon & fabric

body art

Designer: Mikki Livanos

Create the background from stitched patterned paper and a large photo. Create a tag to slide behind the photo and embellish the layout with a stencil letter, bookplate, tag, stickers, fabric and eyelets.

pigtails

Designer: Julie Amber Jones

Wrap a matted photo with different ribbon and patterned paper. Print journaling onto cardstock and finish the background with patterned paper and photos. Embellish the layout with a tag, ink and brads.

always

Designer: Maria Burke

Print journaling onto cardstock and finish the background with inked patterned paper and a matted photo. Embellish the layout with stickers, ribbon tied to twine, a stamp, photo turn and definition.

from paradise

Designer: Me & My Big Ideas

Print a photo onto fabric paper and zigzag stitch to the background. Create the background from crumpled, inked and torn patterned paper. Create a pocket from stitched patterned paper and fill with a sanded and inked postcard. Embellish the layout with stickers, ribbon and a fabric label.

family time

Designer: Marsha Musselman

Print a sketched photo onto cardstock and frame with a ribbon. Print journaling onto patterned paper and attach to the background with rivets. Finish the layout with twine, ribbon, clay, metal embellishments and photos.

can i keep him

Designer: Dana Swords

Create a mini album from cardstock and paint chips, punch holes in the top and attach together with ribbon. Create a window in the cover and place a photo behind the window. Embellish the cover with stamps, patterned paper, mesh, ribbon and a label.

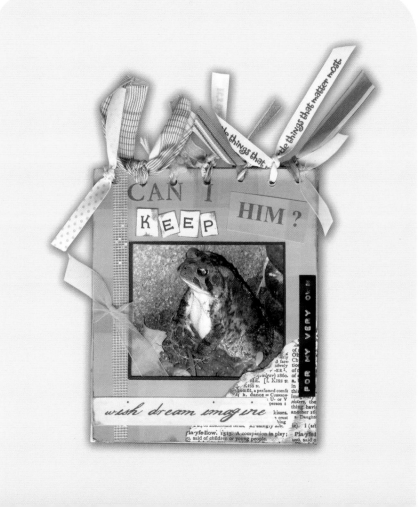

halloween tag

Designer: Melodee Langworthy

Cut a rectangle of white cardstock, wrap with inked gauze and attach black brads for the eyes. Create a tag from inked patterned paper and embellish the tag with a metal clip, bubble embellishment, rickrack, fabric labels and ribbon.

panther

Designer: Karen Buck

Brush ribbon with metallic rub-ons, tie together and adhere to the background between the photos. Create the title from cardstock circles and stickers. Finish the layout with a leather frame.

working with
(7) stickers
& stamps

Did you ever collect stickers when you were younger? I did and kept them neatly stored in a collector's journal never to be used. Twenty years later I'm collecting stickers again, but this time they are being put to good use on scrapbook pages and projects. The variety and availability of stickers have increased over the years and now stickers can be found for just about every possible need or want. Stamps have also made a comeback, finding their way onto almost every scrapbook page and project. Alphabet and image stamps are used prolifically with ink, paint and embossing powder. Take ideas from these pages and projects for use on your own pages.

stickers & stamps

ScrapEssentials JoAnn

trick or treat tag

Designer: Sam Cousins

Create a tag pocket and tag out of patterned paper using a template. Ink the tag and pocket and embellish with a sanded photo, stickers, metal embellishments and ribbon.

ScrapEssentials JoAnn

halloween 2003

Designer: NanC & Company Design

Create the background from inked patterned paper and cardstock. Print the title and journaling onto a transparency and embellish the layout with a matted photo, fiber, eyelets and stickers.

Step 1

Cover a paint can with patterned paper and the lid with cardstock.

Step 2

Paint foam stamps with green and yellow paint and stamp the letters onto cardstock. Cut out each letter, mat with cardstock and adhere to the can.

time capsule

Designer: NanC & Company Design

Step 3

Finish the title with sanded letter stickers and stamps. Print the time capsule instructions onto cardstock, trim in a circle and mat with patterned paper before adhering to the lid.

the boogie board

Designer: Maria Williams

Create the title from cardstock, a foam bookmark and stickers. Print journaling onto cardstock and embellish the layout with photos, ribbon, handwriting, ink and a tag.

little boy card

Designer: Bea Elizalde

Adhere patterned paper, cardstock and stickers to a card and embellish with brads and floss.

pure joy

Designer: Tracy A. Weinzapfel Burgos

Color block the background
with inked cardstock and
patterned paper. Stamp the title
and journaling and embellish
the layout with ribbon, a ribbon
charm and photo.

all about me mini album

Designer: Katie Watson

ScrapEssentials

Create the backgrounds from patterned paper and cardstock. Embellish the
pages with photos, stamps and embellishments.

beach wedding

Designer: Kristi Mangan

Tear and ink a tag and adorn with fiber and a twist tie. Create the title with stickers and the background from patterned paper and a photo. Finish the layout with rub-ons, stickers, a label and metal embellishment.

sweet summer beach babe

Designer: Sharon Laakkonen

Create the background from circles and rectangles of inked patterned paper. Create the title with stickers and stamps and embellish the layout with rub-ons, ribbon, leather bookplates and a flower.

fear factor
Designer: Rachael Giallongo

Stamp the title onto cardstock, trim, mat and finish with letter stencils. Create the background from stitched patterned paper and cardstock and embellish the layout with paint, ribbon, brads and a vellum tag.

how granddads survive
Designer: Monique Mclean

Create the title from mailbox letters and letter stickers. Create the background from patterned paper, cardstock and a photo and finish the layout with labels and stickers.

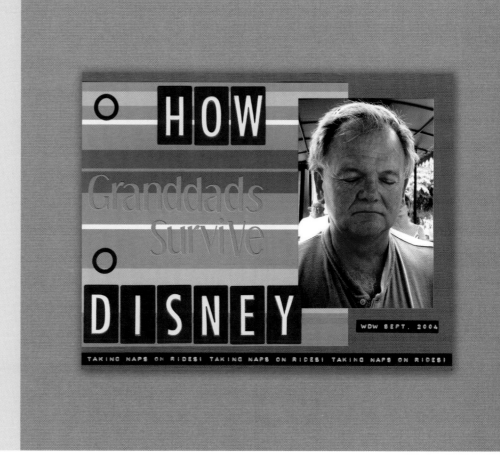

stickers & stamps

a boy and his

teddy bear

Kai received this snow white teddy bear from Great grandpa and Great grandma as a gift for his birth. Since then, this teddy is Kai's good buddy. He plays, cuddles and sleeps with teddy all the time. July 2004

a boy and his teddy bear

Designer: Yukari Coxwell

Print journaling onto patterned paper and create the background from patterned paper. Embellish the layout with photos, stickers, buttons and metal corners.

inking

Scrapbookers and paper crafters have found a variety of uses for inkpads in addition to rubber stamping. Inkpads are often used with embossing powder, to create borders around pages and to create vintage looks.

There are three kinds of inkpads: pigment based, dye based and solvent based. Pigment based ink is recommended for scrapbooking purposes because they come in vibrant colors, can be used on many different mediums, dry slowly making them great for embossing and, most importantly, they are fade resistant. Dye based ink dries quickly and works better on coated paper than pigment based ink, but will bleed on absorbent paper. Solvent based ink is designed for decorative use on non-porous surfaces and is great on wood, metal, glass, cellophane, leather and more. We have found solvent and pigment based ink work well for crafting purposes.

Most inkpads are archival safe, but check the packaging just to make sure. Most inkpads can be re-inked if the

inkpad has become dry, just follow the re-inking directions to refill your inkpad. For the inkpad to last longer, be sure to replace the cap tightly after each use and store your ink upside down.

Ideas for inking:

- Brush different colors of ink onto a stamp to create a multicolored image on your project
- Lightly brush an inkpad over cardstock, paper and embellishments for a finished look
- Sprinkle embossing powder or Ultra Thick Embossing Enamel (UTEE) over a stamped image, shake off the excess powder and heat emboss
- Dab ink over a template to create an image (you can create your own templates cut or punched from cardstock)
- Add dimension to your projects by inking cardstock, photos, tags, metals and other embellishments

amelia & mommy

Designer: Alison M. Lockett

Stamp a decorative stamp around a matted photo. Print the journaling and title onto patterned paper, sand the edges and adhere to the background. Embellish the layout with ribbon, staples and a letter stencil.

dancing girl

Designer: Tracy A. Weinzapfel Burgos

Stamp the title onto cardstock and finish the title with inked letter stickers. Create the background from patterned paper, cardstock and photos. Embellish the layout with ribbon, ink and a metal bookplate.

seasons greetings card

Designer: Pam Canavan

Embellish a card with patterned paper, stickers, metal embellishments and a 3-D embellishment.

holiday wishes tin and cd ornaments

Designer: Michele Edgley

Cover a tin with patterned paper, stickers and ribbon and embellish CDs with photos, twine, ribbon and stickers.

97   building blocks

Scrap **Essentials** Jo-Ann

christmas joy

Designer: Pam Canavan

Sand patterned paper and embellish the page with a photo, ribbon and stickers.

Scrap **Essentials** Jo-Ann

adios card

Designer: Bea Elizalde

Thread fiber through stickers and attach to cardstock. Finish the card with patterned paper and brads.

stickers & stamps

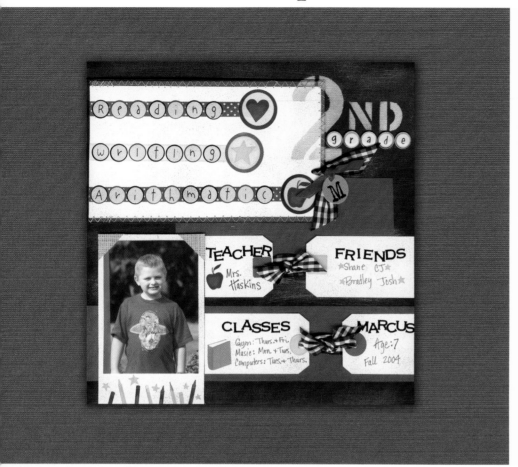

2nd grade

Designer: Marsha Musselman

Create a flap from stitched cardstock and create a paper hinge so the flap can fold back to reveal what is underneath. Create the background from painted cardstock and tie tags together with ribbon. Finish the layout with stamps, stickers, metal letters, a photo and handwriting.

all these things and more

Designer: Li'l Davis Designs

Stamp the title onto cardstock with black and red ink, stamping one letter onto red paper. Create the background from cardstock, brads, ribbon, a photo and metal bookplate. Finish the layout with crushed bottle caps strung with string.

stamping

Stamping is not limited to rubber stamps and inkpads anymore. You can stamp with paint, embossing powder, ink pens, foam stamps, letter stamps, homemade stamps, date stamps, magnetic stamps and more. Perform a test on a scratch piece of paper before stamping directly onto your project. Be sure to clean your stamps after each use so they will last a long time.

Ideas for stamping:

- Ink one stamp with different color inkpads
- After stamping an image, re-stamp lightly just to the side of the stamp to create a shadow
- Use the cutout of a decorative punch as a stamp
- Make homemade stamps from potatoes and sponges

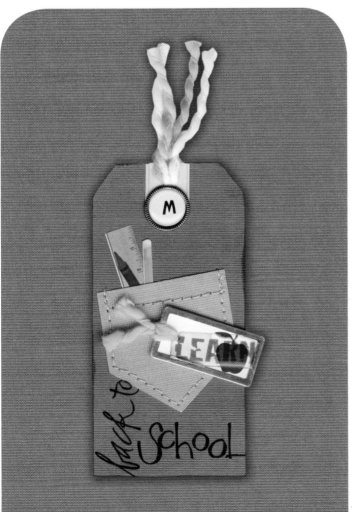

ScrapEssentials Jo-Ann

back to school tag

Designer: Marsha Musselman

Make a pocket from stitched cardstock and fill with stickers. Create a tag from cardstock and embellish with rub-ons, fiber, metal embellishments, stickers, ink and a bubble.

little girl
Designer: Katerina McLane

Create the background from torn and inked patterned paper and a photo. Stamp the title and corner decoration. Finish the layout with ribbon, flowers, hinges, snaps and a brad.

ScrapEssentials JoAnn

school time
Designer: Tristann Graves

Create the background from inked patterned paper and slide report cards behind the patterned paper. Mat one photo and adhere a smaller photo onto a tag. Embellish the layout with stickers, rub-ons, metal embellishments, ribbon, rickrack and a transparency.

legend of a grandpa

Designer: Ginger Ditton

Print title and journaling onto cardstock, trim and mat. Create the background from patterned paper, cardstock, metal mesh, photos and stitching. Embellish the layout with stamps, letter stencils, twine, nail heads and a metal bookplate.

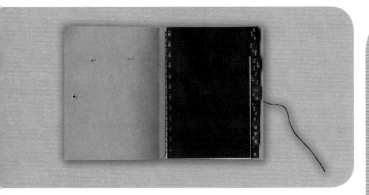

address book

Designer: Colorbok, Inc.

Fold cardboard to create a book cover and cover with patterned paper. Stamp letters onto black cardstock for the divider pages and print address sheets onto white cardstock. Bind the address sheets and black dividers together and adhere to the back cover. Embellish the book with patterned paper, stamps, string and a metal bookplate.

stickers
& stamps

ScrapEssentials™

a thing of beauty
file folder card

Designer: Anna Estrada Davison

Cover a mini file folder with patterned paper and embellish the outside and inside with stickers, ribbon, metal embellishments, a photo, tag, pocket and flower.

how?

Designer: Shelly Umbanhowar

Stamp the title onto patterned paper and the journaling onto a tag. Create the background from patterned paper and photos. Embellish the layout with rub-ons, ribbon and ink.

creature specs

Designer: Kerry Umbanhowar

Create the background from inked patterned paper and cardstock. Slide a tag behind the photo and finish the layout with stickers, stamps, rub-ons, staples and ribbon.

real love

Designer: Melissa Koehler

Mat a photo with cardstock and cardboard and paint the edges of the photo. Stamp the title onto a transparency and outline "love" with red paint. Embellish the layout with printed journaling, brads, a flower and label.

working with

(8) envelopes
& tags

Our designers have outdone themselves with unique ways to use tags and envelopes in this section. Notice the gift card made from an envelope, the many tags hidden cleverly behind photos or the tag pocket album made from envelopes. The ideas in this section showcase just a few of the many uses envelopes and tags can have on your projects. We hope they will inspire you to come up with new ways to use these versatile supplies.

moments
of solitude

Designer: Briana Fisher

Rip a corner out of patterned paper and adhere to cardstock. Handwrite the journaling onto cardstock, attach a photo to the background with photo corners and finish the layout with a tag, twine and rub-ons.

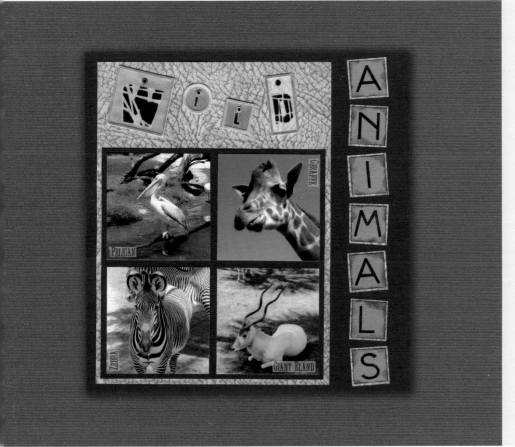

ScrapEssentials Jo-Ann

wild animals

Designer: NanC & Company Design

Create the title from metal-rimmed tags, letter stickers and printed cardstock. Finish the layout with photos, ink and printed vellum.

canada tag

Designer: Marsha Musselman

Sand a black tag and embellish it with tags, stickers, ribbon, 3-D embellishments, metal embellishments and a letter stencil.

miss u card

Designer: Shannon Bastian

Attach mini tags to patterned paper with ribbon and embellish the card with patterned paper, rub-ons, floss, a button and flower.

envelopes & tags

the simple things

Designer: Leisure Arts, Inc.

Create the background from a collage of patterned paper and photos. Create the title from letter stickers and patterned paper and print the journaling onto cardstock. Embellish the layout with a tag, sticker, eyelets, fiber and ink.

Scrap Essentials JoAnn

little champion

Designer: Wendy Malichio

Walnut ink four tags, tape together and print the title onto the tags. Scan the ribbon award, reduce the size, cut out and adhere to the background. Create the background from inked patterned paper, cardstock and a large photo. Embellish the layout with ribbon, fiber and metal embellishments.

brothers

Designer: Marsha Musselman

Create the title and journaling from metal-rimmed tags. Embellish the layout with metal bars, stickers, paint, handwriting, twine and brads.

autumn tag

Designer: Rachael Giallongo

Ink a tag and embellish it with patterned paper, ribbon, definitions, staples, a photo, brad and leaf.

gratitude tag

Designer: Rachael Giallongo

Create a flap from cardstock and patterned paper and attach to the tag with metal hinges. Finish the tag with stickers, metal embellishments, ribbon, fiber and a definition.

envelopes & tags

concerts
cd case book

Designer: Colorbok, Inc.

Cover the inside of a CD case and a CD with patterned paper. Accordion fold the same patterned paper and adhere vellum envelopes to the folds to create a tag book. Fill the envelopes with concert tickets and embellish the book.

ScrapEssentials Jo-Ann

butte, montana

Designer: Katie Watson

Ink the edge of a vellum envelope and fill with a metal-rimmed tag adorned with stickers and ribbon. Create the background from sanded, inked and torn patterned paper and cardstock. Embellish the layout with a framed photo, vellum quote, flower, photo corners, handwriting and stamps.

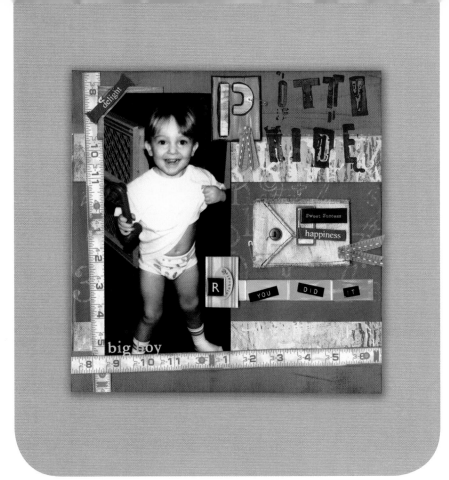

potty pride

Designer: Wendy Malichio

Ink a canvas envelope and embellish it with fabric labels, ribbon, staples and a metal-rimmed tag. Create the background from inked patterned paper, cardstock, measuring tape and a photo. Embellish the layout with a 3-D embellishment, letter stencil, paint chip, paint, stamps, stickers, ribbon, fabric labels and safety pins.

pockets

Pockets add a sense of fun and anticipation to a page or project. They are perfect for hiding personal journaling and are a fun place to hold maps, letters, tickets and gift cards. Pockets are a great addition to activity books for children, as well, because they love removing photos and surprises from pockets.

Ideas for pockets:

- Turn envelopes into pockets
- Sew fabric onto a page or project as a pocket
- Sew a sheet of vellum to the bottom of a page and sew vertical lines to create many vellum pockets
- Fold cardstock to form a pocket
- Create an expandable pocket with accordion sides
- Fill pockets with tags, photos, notes and more

envelopes & tags

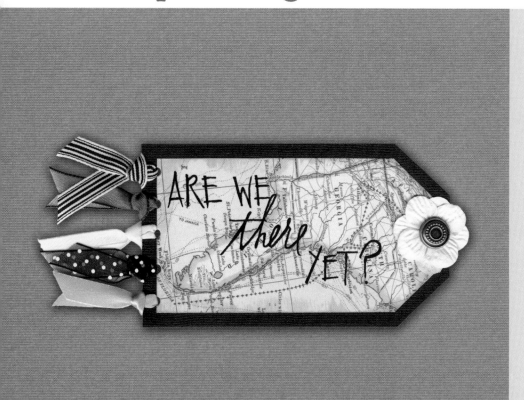

are we there yet? tag

Designer: Nicole Jackson

Create a tag from patterned paper and cardstock. Embellish the tag with ribbon, rub-ons, a flower and metal embellishment.

gift card envelope

Designer: Bea Elizalde

ScrapEssentials JoAnn

Fold a standard envelope in half and cut the flap down the middle. Decorate the inside and outside of the envelope with patterned paper and embellish the envelope with metal embellishments, stickers, fiber, ribbon and cardstock.

grandpa

Designer: Natalie Quandt

Create the journaling from distressed tags, rub-ons, metals and a quote. Embellish the layout with a sanded and matted photo, fiber, ink and metal embellishments.

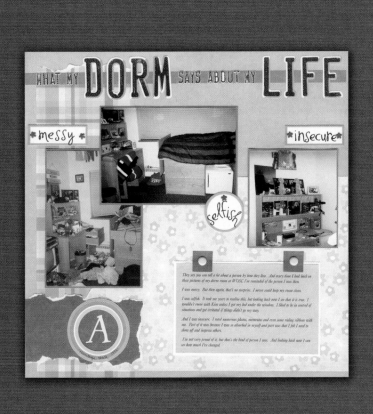

dorm life

Designer: Annette Pixley

Create the background from patterned paper, cardstock and photos. Print journaling onto patterned paper and create the title from letter stickers. Embellish the layout with tags, rub-ons and brads.

girlish charm

Designer: Karen Buck

Create a tag flip booklet from laminated pouches filled with photos and journaling. Attach the booklet to a mini page with a metal ring, eyelets and ribbon. Embellish the mini page with a tag sticker, flower sticker covered with micro beads, ink and ribbon.

pepsi

Designer: Miranda Isenberg

Print journaling onto cardstock and cut in the shape of a file folder to hide behind the photo. Create the background from patterned paper, cardstock and a photo. Fill a vellum envelope with a letter and embellish the layout with letter stickers and tiles.

aubrey

Designer: Me & My Big Ideas

Create the background and a pocket from stitched patterned paper. Print journaling onto paper, mat and adhere an embellishment to the top. Fill the pocket with tags made from patterned paper, rub-ons and ribbon.

three boys

Designer: Tarri Botwinski

Paint the edges of metal-rimmed tags. Create the background from patterned paper, cardstock and a photo. Finish the layout with stickers, ribbon, brads, stitched patterned paper and metal embellishments.

for you tag

Designer: Miranda Isenberg

Create a tag from cardstock and patterned paper and embellish the tag with stamps, ribbon, brads, a vellum envelope and tile.

magic happens

Designer: Wanda E. Santiago-Cintron

Create the title from metal letters, labels, paint and a tag. Create the background from patterned paper and a matted photo. Embellish the layout with ribbon photo corners, brads, labels, ribbon, ink and a vellum quote.

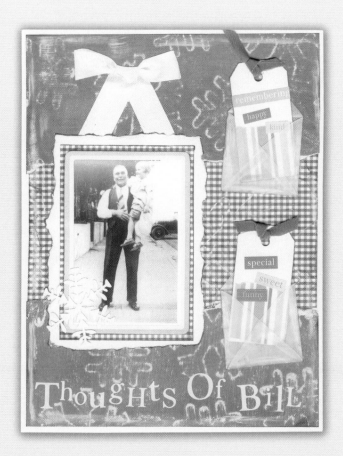

thoughts of bill

Designer: Katie Watson

Place snowflake die cuts behind blue paper and sand until the edges of the snowflakes appear. Create the background from sanded, inked and painted paper and cardstock. Finish the layout with inked and painted vellum envelopes, tags, stickers, ribbon, a die cut and photo.

ScrapEssentials

loved 4 ever

Designer: Keisha Campbell

Ink tags, cover with
transparencies and embellish
with ribbon, stamps, paint and
metal embellishments. Create
the background from inked
patterned paper, cardstock and
a photo. Finish the layout with
flowers, letter stickers, a metal
brad, acrylic flower and
letter stencil.

ScrapEssentials

nyc

Designer: Leisure Arts, Inc.

Create the background from
stitched patterned paper, photos
and a postcard. Create a tag
from patterned paper, cardstock,
stitching, letter stickers and fiber.

candy crazy

Designer: Robin Middendorf

Create the title from inked letters and tags and finish with ribbon. Create the background from patterned paper, photos and ribbon. Slide a tag with journaling behind a photo and embellish the layout with letter stickers, ribbon and a flower.

ScrapEssentials JoAnn

accordion tag book

Designer: Susan Stringfellow

Create an accordion tag book from cardstock. Embellish with patterned paper, photos, fiber and embellishments.

envelopes & tags

just relax

Designer: Monica Kornfeld

Fill a mini file folder with journaling printed onto patterned paper. Create the background from inked patterned paper and cardstock. Mat a photo with a collage of patterned paper stitched to cardstock. Embellish the layout with brads, photo corners, stickers, patterned paper, ribbon, a metal clip and file folder label.

live

Designer: Tammy Gauck

Adhere a large photo to patterned paper and embellish with a tag, fiber and rub-ons.

traditions
at the pool

Designer: Sam Cousins

Fold pieces of yellow cardstock in half, adhere the backs to the background and photos to the fronts. Fill the insides with journaling. Create the background from patterned paper and cardstock and finish the layout with metal embellishments, tags, ribbon and handwriting.

scooter girl

Designer: Gimi Willie

Create the background from patterned paper, cardstock, frame stickers and photos. Print journaling onto a transparency and embellish the layout with stickers, metal letters, ribbon, ink and metal-rimmed tags.

1st cream cone

Designer: Sam Cousins

Create the background from patterned paper, photos and tags. Embellish the layout with stickers, stamps, ribbon, staples and a cork tag.

in the blink of an eye

Designer: Diana Furey

Create the title from tags, patterned paper, metal embellishments, rub-ons and ribbon. Print the journaling onto a transparency and adhere to the background over fabric and rickrack. Embellish the layout with a photo, slide mount, stamps and metal embellishments.

Step 1

Fill a frame with cardstock adhered to patterned paper.

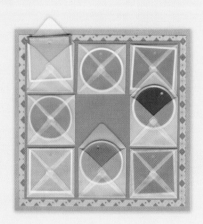

Step 2

Adhere eight vellum envelopes to the cardstock and fill the envelopes with metal-rimmed tags.

Jo-Ann
ScrapEssentials

kimble & kara frame

Designer: NanC & Company Design

Step 3

Adhere photos to the metal-rimmed tags, print the subject of each photo onto cardstock and trim in the shape of a tag. Attach the tags to the photos with floss. Create the title from letter stickers and handwriting.

working with
9 buttons, bubbles & tiles

Buttons, bubbles and tiles are commonly used as accents on pages and projects. Buttons add a homemade feel, bubbles add dimension and shine and tiles add flare, pattern and color to a page or project. In this section, notice how tiles have been embellished with rub-ons and cut to create mosaics and photo corners. Notice how buttons have been used as flower centers and how bubbles have been used to highlight words and cover tags. Use buttons, bubbles and tiles to add color and dimension to your projects.

buttons, bubbles & tiles

journaling

Journaling is one of the most important ways to preserve memories. It allows us to record dates, people, places, events, thoughts, feelings and memories. Many of us fear journaling, but that fear can be overcome with a few simple ideas.

- Take time to find your own personal journaling style. You might like to make lists, quote people directly, write letters to the viewer or write a detailed summary of what happened. Experiment with different styles until you find one that fits for you.
- Keep a notebook with you upon which you can write ideas for journaling or direct quotes of a loved one.
- Write in the present tense instead of the past.
- Have a brainstorming session writing everything that comes to your mind about a person or event.
- Use a quote, poem or the lyrics of a song to convey your thoughts.

Ideas for journaling:

- Handwrite
- Use computer fonts to print:
  - directly onto a page
  - onto cardstock
  - onto vellum or a transparency
  - onto fabric
- Stitch journaling with floss
- Form wire into letters and words
- Use stickers, metal letters and rub-ons

- Ask a child, husband or friend to write what they remember about an event or tradition.
- Summarize your memories of a year in a few sentences.

Don't forget to include yourself in your scrapbooks and journaling. Create a page all about you and include your personal insights, what you love to do, funny quirks about you, etc. If you are concerned about other people viewing personal journaling, hide journaling on tags behind photos or in envelopes and pockets.

our european vacation

Designer: NanC & Company Design

Print journaling onto vellum, fill in the gaps with metallic words and highlight other words with bubbles. Mat photos with cardstock and patterned paper and finish the layout with tiles, floss, brads and a metallic phrase.

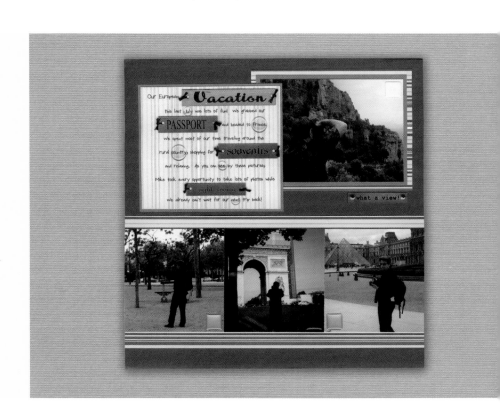

Step 1

Cover a recipe box and lid with cardstock.

Step 2

Adhere patterned paper to one corner of the box and ribbon around the bottom of the box. Attach buttons to the lid in a wavy line with pop dots.

ScrapEssentials Jo-Ann

recipe box

Designer: NanC & Company Design

Step 3

Embellish the box with letter stickers, bubbles and metal letters.

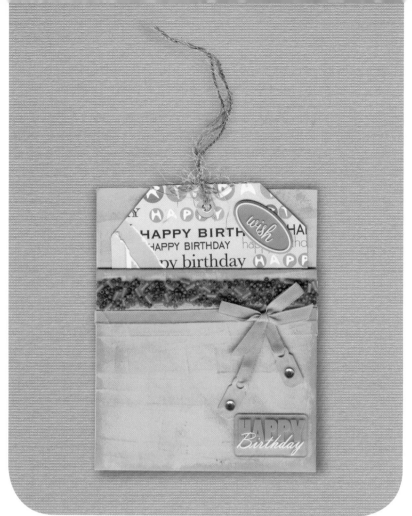

birthday wish
pocket and tag

Designer: Randi Lanz

Adorn a library card pocket with ink, beads, ribbon, tags and a jelly label. Adhere torn patterned paper to the tag and embellish it with a vellum quote, jelly label, fiber, ribbon and gems.

nikki notepad

Designer: Miranda Isenberg

Cover a notepad with patterned paper and embellish the notepad with a vellum envelope, ribbon and tiles embellished with rub-ons.

Scrap**Essentials** Jo-Ann

mom mini album
Designer: Miranda Isenberg

Cut tabs from poster board
and adhere to pages of an
old children's book. Paint the
book, adhere patterned paper
to the pages and modge podge
the book. Adorn the book
with photos, ribbon, tags and
embellishments.

Scrap**Essentials** Jo-Ann

scrapper's block idea jar
Designer: Miranda Isenberg

Print the title onto cardstock and adhere the
title and patterned paper to a canning jar.
Embellish the jar with ribbon and tiles and fill
the jar with scrapbooking ideas printed onto
strips of cardstock.

buttons, bubbles & tiles

heart breaker

Designer: Kerry Umbanhowar

Create the background from inked patterned paper and cardstock. Adhere a photo leaving space for journaling to slide behind the photo. Embellish the layout with buttons, ribbon, stickers, metal embellishments, a clear tag and label.

grandma's tackle box

Designer: Michelle Hubbartt

Thread buttons with floss and adhere to netting. Create the background from distressed patterned paper, cardstock and photos. Embellish the layout with metal embellishments, negative photo frames, ribbon, letters, journaling printed onto a transparency and labels.

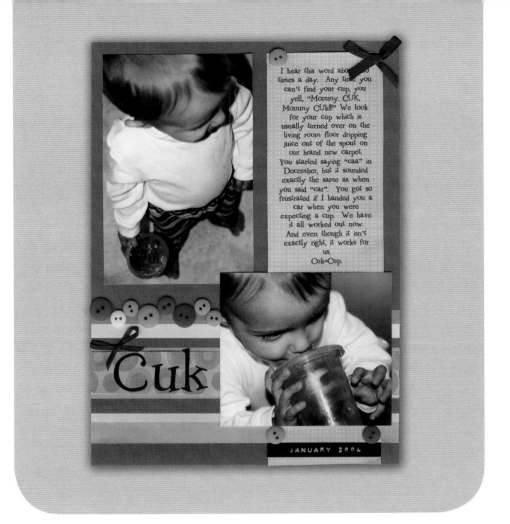

cuk

Designer: Robin Middendorf

Print journaling onto patterned paper and create the background from patterned paper. Embellish the layout with photos, buttons, letter stickers, ribbon and a label.

flower card

Designer: Michele Edgley

Create a gatefold card from patterned paper. Cut a pot from cardstock and create a flower and stem from ribbon. Finish the card with a button, floss, chalk and letter stickers.

buttons, bubbles & tiles

home movies

Designer: Teri Anderson

Cut a tile in half diagonally for unique photo corners. Dry brush black cardstock with acrylic paint and stamp the title. Adhere photos of movies and journaling to the background framed by an overlay. Finish the layout with stickers and tiles.

holiday greetings card

Designer: NanC & Company Design

Cut tiles and create a candy cane mosaic. Sand and ink cardstock for the background and finish the card with handwriting, brads, fiber, patterned paper and bubbles.

Mosaics are a unique way to accent pages and projects. A mosaic is made by combining small pieces of a material in various colors to make patterns and images. Just cut paper, photos or embellishments and adhere to a background forming a pattern.

Ideas for mosaics:

- Cut pieces of cardstock and patterned paper for a mosaic
- Cut tiles and bubbles for a mosaic
- Cut doubles of photos and arrange in a mosaic
- Cut thin metal and acrylic pieces for a mosaic

ScrapEssentials Jo-Ann

live it boy style

Designer: Wendy Malichio

Create the background from inked patterned paper, painted cardstock and a scratched photo. Cover a mini manila envelope with cardstock and monogrammed patterned paper and fill the envelope with printed journaling. Embellish the layout with stickers, bubbles, mesh, ribbon and a bookplate.

buttons, bubbles & tiles

freedom

Designer: Julie Laakso

Create the background from stitched cardstock and attach cardstock and photos to the left side of the page with brads. Print journaling onto cardstock and hide behind the photos. Embellish the layout with rub-ons, buttons, floss, beads and bubbles.

i love you card

Designer: Lisa M. Thayer

Create the title from alphabet buttons and the background from patterned paper, cardstock, brads and a slide mount.

red, white, blue and you

Designer: Heather Dewaelsche

Flatten the back of star brads and use as unique photo corners. Create the title from alphabet buttons, stamped paper and metal letters. Create the background from sanded patterned paper, cardstock and photos. Embellish the layout with metal embellishments, ribbon, vellum journaling and a tag.

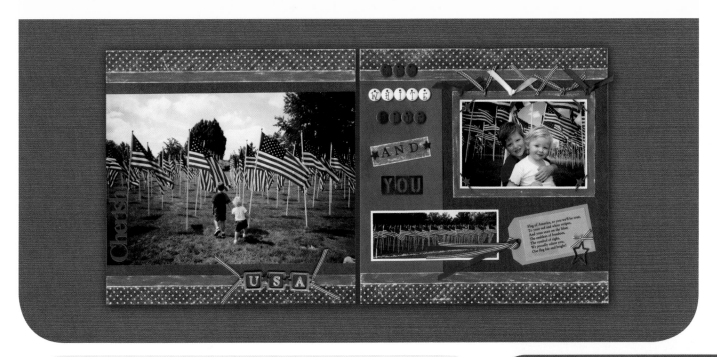

chill factor

Designer: Creative Imaginations

Create the background from patterned paper, cardstock and photos. Print journaling onto cardstock, adhere to the background and finish the layout with stickers.

buttons, bubbles & tiles

she's got a way about her
Designer: Annette Pixley

Create the background from inked and stitched patterned paper. Mat a photo with inked cardstock and embellish the layout with ribbon, photo turns, bubbles, frames, a leather flower, quote and button.

sunsets and sandcastles
Designer: Tammy Gauck

Create the title from stamps, bubble letters and a transparency. Create the background from patterned paper and a photo and finish the layout with flowers, an eyelet and button.

sweetie pie

Designer: Andrea Mette

Paint the centers of flowers with paint and cover the paint with bubbles. Create the background from crumpled and inked patterned paper and a painted photo. Stamp the title and embellish the layout with a vintage label, safety pin, paint, ribbon and staples.

you are

Designer: Cassonda Tadlock

Create a collage of patterned paper, stitching and inked cardstock for the background. Mat a photo and attach to the background with metal photo corners. Create the title from stickers, bubbles and stamps and finish the layout with transparencies, flowers and a tag.

buttons,
bubbles
& tiles

thinking of you
matchbook card

Designer: Rachael Giallongo

Create a matchbook card from
patterned paper and embellish
it with staples, stamps, floss, a
flower and button.

ice cream fun

Designer: Cindy Smith

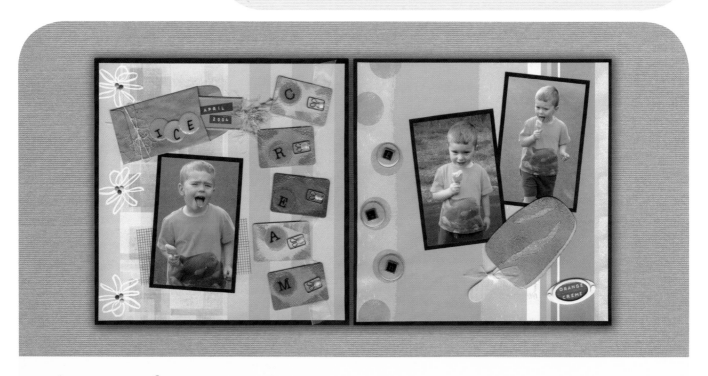

Heat emboss formica samples with Ultra Thick Embossing Enamel (UTEE) and repeat for a wet look. Cover
letter stickers with micro beads and thread formica samples with ribbon and paper clips. Cover page pebbles
with letter stickers and cover metal letters with watch crystals. Finish the layout with patterned paper, cardstock,
photos, metal embellishments, labels, fiber, ribbon, a rounded stick and envelope.

swim

Designer: Brandy Brandon

Create a collage of patterned paper for the background. Print journaling onto vellum and attach to the layout with brads. Embellish the layout with a matted photo, stickers, metal-rimmed tags, floss and buttons.

slip-n-slide

Designer: Annette Pixley

Create the background from patterned paper, cardstock and photos. Embellish the layout with bubbles, stickers, stamps, a flower and brad.

true love

f

LOVE

I

H

2005

JAN 1st 2005

CELEBRATE

C

happy

k

m

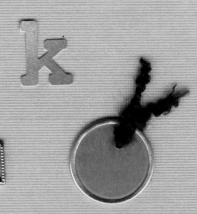

A

N

CHERISH

working with
10 metals

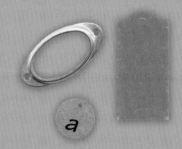

Can you remember what scrapbooking was like before metals? This one element has dramatically changed the way we scrapbook. Paper crafters have turned to hardware stores to find hinges, washers, frame holders and staples for their projects. Scrapbooking and craft stores are also full of metal embellishments specifically made for crafting purposes. Except for being archival safe, there are no rules when it comes to using metals, so search your home and stores to find metals that will dazzle your pages.

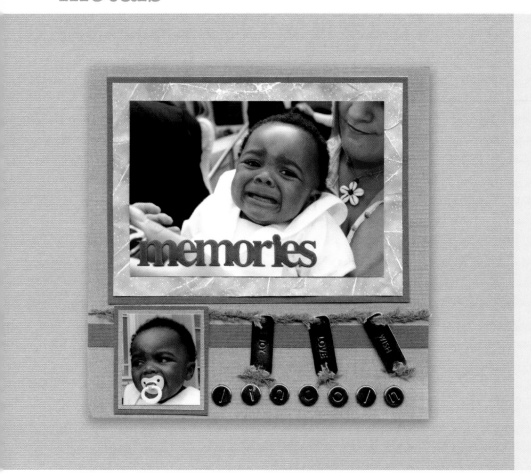

memories

Designer: NanC & Company Design

Sand a metal word and adhere it to the photo. Mat photos with cardstock and crumpled and sanded patterned paper. Embellish the layout with fiber, metal words and letters.

wish upon a star

Designer: Sandra Liddell

Thread a metal word with ribbon and tie pieces of a thinner ribbon onto the thicker ribbon. Create the background from inked patterned paper, cardstock and a photo. Finish the layout with handwritten journaling, brads, a sticker and a metal bookplate.

sandpaper

Sandpaper is a favorite tool of many paper crafters. It is easy to use and new ways to alter embellishments and paper with sandpaper are constantly being discovered.

Sandpaper can be purchased at home improvement stores and craft stores. Sandpaper usually comes as a thin sheet of paper, but we have also found sandpaper attached to a sponge which makes it easier to handle and use. A medium grit (80-120 grit) sandpaper works well for paper crafting, but a fine (150+ grit) or coarse (40-60 grit) paper will work as well. A finer sandpaper will create more lines that don't penetrate the paper or metal as deeply as the coarser sandpaper and the coarser sandpaper will have less lines and penetrate deeper.

Ideas for sanding:

- Sand textured cardstock with a white core to have a little bit of the white show through
- Crumple and ink paper and then sand to remove some of the ink and have the ridges of the paper weathered
- Sand metal and metallic embellishments including letters, words, brads, eyelets, frames and tags

my family

Designer: Kristi Mangan

Create the background from inked patterned paper, cardstock and a photo. Thread ribbon through metal words and adhere to the cardstock. Create the title from letter and number stickers and embellish the layout with ribbon and staples.

metals

girlie girl
Designer: Caroline Huot

Attach flowers to the background with metal brads. Fold cardstock in half as a photo mat, scrap the inside with journaling and photos and keep the flap down with photo turns. Create the background from patterned paper and cardstock. Embellish the layout with paint, ribbon, stamps, rub-ons, stars and handwriting.

sisters
Designer: Susan Weinroth

Stamp the title and journaling and attach the journaling to the page with photo turns. Create the background from patterned paper and a photo. Finish the layout with ribbon, tags, ink, and metal embellishments.

memories

Designer: Susan Weinroth

Mat a photo with stitched fabric
and attach the photo to the
fabric with photo turns and brads.
Create the background from inked
patterned paper and cardstock.
Ink the title letters and print
journaling onto cardstock and ink.
Finish the layout with ribbon, metal
embellishments, a flower and tag.

confidence

Designer: Kerry Umbanhowar

Create the background from
inked patterned paper and
cardstock. Mat a photo and
embellish the layout with
ribbon, staples, stickers, rub-
ons and metal photo corners.

smile

Designer: Melissa Koehler

Photographer: Stacie Koehler

Paint a metal molding strip and adhere to the background separating the cardstock and patterned paper. Mat a photo and embellish the layout with stamped journaling, wood letters, ribbon, safety pins and a frame.

come out and play

Designer: Laura H. McKinley

Cut around a pattern in patterned paper with a craft knife and slide a large photo under the cut out. Embellish the layout with painted metal molding, wire, letter tags, ink and rub-ons.

dreams

Designer: Kathlene Clark

Print black and white photos
and distress the edges with
sandpaper and ink. Create
the background from inked
patterned paper and cardstock.
Finish the layout with fiber,
acrylic words and metal
embellishments.

family mini
heritage album

Designer: Arlana Patten

Create a mini album from
patterned paper and cardstock.
Fold paper like an accordion for
the binding and place two pieces
of cardstock in-between each fold
of the accordion. Punch holes
through the paper and cardstock
and bind with ribbon.

metals

believe
mini journal

Designer: Randi Lanz

Cover a journal with patterned
paper and trim the excess paper
with a craft knife. Rub the spine
with metallic rub-ons and embellish
the journal with fabric, ribbon, fiber,
metal embellishments and an
acrylic word.

inspirational
journal

Designer: Colorbok, Inc.

Cover a cardboard journal
with patterned paper and
embellish the journal with
ribbon, metal embellishments,
stitching and paper.

wished for this

Designer: Elizabeth Cuzzacrea

Create the background from cardstock, patterned paper and a photo. Embellish the layout with a canvas phrase, tag, envelope, label, metal embellishments, ribbon, leather flowers, clay phrases and ink.

magnetic calendar

Designer: Colorbok, Inc.

Adhere patterned paper over a magnetic canvas to create a calendar. Stamp the months, weekdays and dates onto the patterned paper. Cut out the dates in squares, leaving the months and weekdays in the shape of an L. Put magnetic strips behind metal bookplates to highlight the month and day.

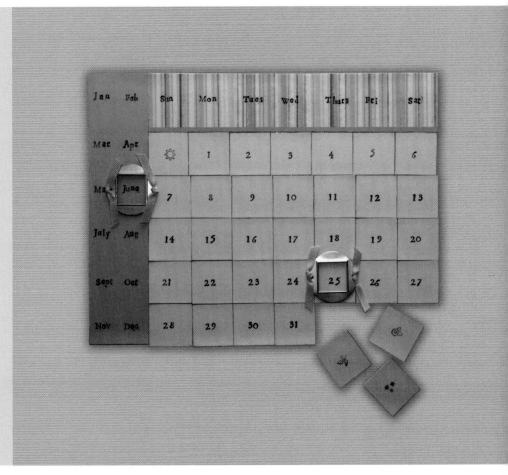

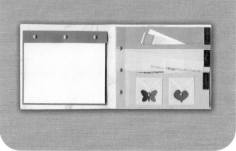

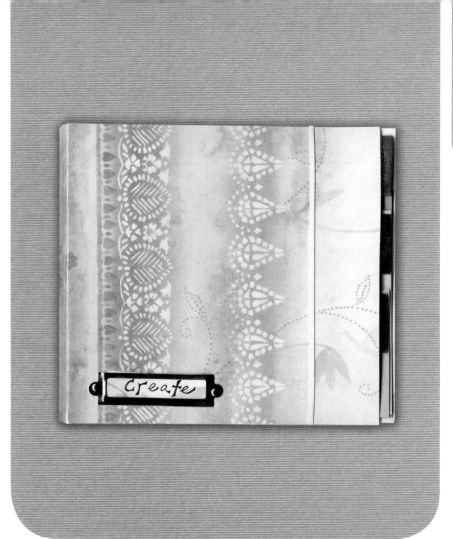

create
pocket journal

Designer: Colorbok, Inc.

Cover poster board with patterned paper to make the cover of a book. Create pockets from cardstock and a notepad from cardstock and paper for the inside. Embellish the journal with metal embellishments and vellum envelopes and quotes. Keep the journal closed with elastic string attached to the back of the journal with an eyelet.

winter
coaster magnet

Designer: Susan Stringfellow

Cover a cardboard coaster with patterned paper and adhere a magnet to the back of the coaster. Embellish the coaster with metal embellishments, clear buttons backed with patterned paper, a cardstock label and crocheted yarn.

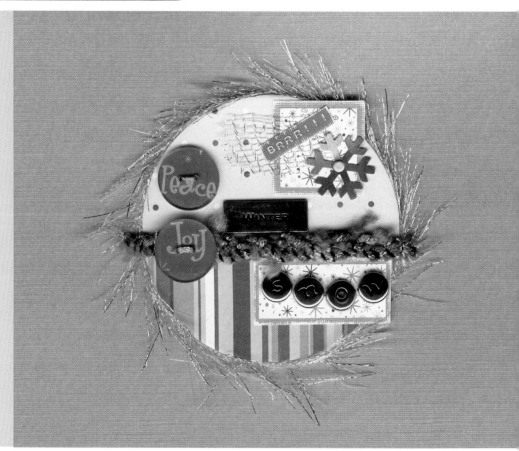

Step 1

Adhere torn and inked cardstock to a notebook cover.

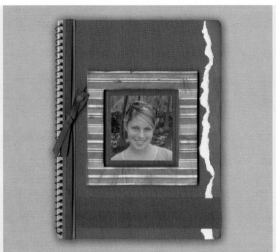

Step 2

Cut out a cardboard frame, cover it with patterned paper and ink the frame. Mat a photo and adhere inside the frame. Wrap ribbon next to the binding of the notebook.

ScrapEssentials JoAnn

my life at 16 journal

Designer: NanC & Company Design

Step 3

Rub letters onto metal tags, mat the circular tags with cardstock and finish the title with letter stickers and bubble letters. Back bubbles with inked patterned paper and adhere to ribbon tied to the frame. Frame tiles with metal conchos, mat with cardstock and adhere to the top right corner of the notebook. Embellish the layout with a metal bookplate and brads.

metals

ScrapEssentials JoAnn

mom gift wrap and tag

Designer: Leah Fung

Paint a metal flower with acrylic paint and attach to a tag with a brad. Embellish the tag with stitching, letters and a safety pin. Wrap a box with patterned paper, tie with a bow and attach the tag to the box with raffia.

paint

A little bit of paint can go a long way in transforming the look of a page or project. Paint is a great tool for paper crafters because it can achieve many different looks, can be used on many different objects and is inexpensive to buy.

Acrylic and watercolor paints are commonly used with paper crafting. They dry quickly, can be cleaned up with water and are archival safe. The paints are available at most craft stores in a range of colors. For most paper crafting purposes a low to medium quality of paint is sufficient.

Acrylic paint can be used on most any object including fabric, paper, wood, metal, canvas and stickers. Watercolor paint is best used on thick paper or canvas. Feel free to apply the paint any way you like, for example, use fingers, brushes, rags, sponges or stamps.

Ideas for painting:

- Create a wash of color with watercolors or with watered down acrylics
- Use watercolors for bright, almost transparent colors
- Use acrylics in matte, glossy and crackle finishes
- Layer acrylics on top of one another for dimension
- Sand acrylic paint after it has dried for a weathered look
- Stamp images and letters with paint, just be sure to clean your stamps when you are done

love card and tag

Designer: Nicole Jackson

Lightly paint metal embellishments and finish the card and tag with torn patterned paper, cardstock, rub-ons, ribbon and tags.

keaton bug

Designer: Diana Furey

Create the background from cardstock, patterned paper and a transparency. Tie ribbon down the side of a matted photo and embellish the layout with painted metals, letter tiles, ribbon and slide mounts.

metals

memories box

Designer: Lisa M. Thayer

Cover a box and lid with patterned paper and adhere a metal word to the top of the lid.

celebrate card and envelope

Designer: Colorbok, Inc.

Create the envelope from stitched patterned paper and the card from cardstock and stitched patterned paper. Embellish the card and envelope with metal embellishments, handwriting and a vellum quote.

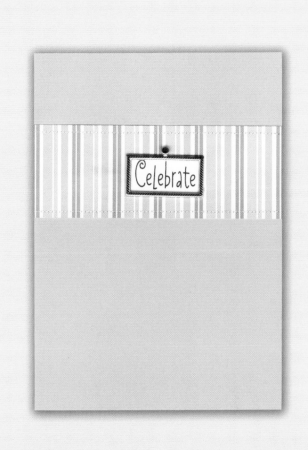

cody & goofy

Designer: Linda Beeson

Create the background from stitched patterned paper. Mat photos and embellish the layout with stickers, stitching and metal embellishments.

buds

Designer: Krista Fernandez

Create the background from patterned paper and cardstock. Stamp with paint and embellish the layout with photos and metal embellishments.

you inspire me to be tag

Designer: Sam Cousins

Adhere metal words over metal bookplates and onto a vellum envelope. Create a tag from patterned paper and cardstock and embellish the tag with ribbon, fiber and handwriting.

e i e i o

Designer: Johanna Peterson

Mat a photo with chicken wire and embellish the wire with ribbon, metal embellishments, tags, flowers, tiny clothespins and a letter stencil. Create the background from stitched cardstock and finish the layout with ribbon, rub-ons, safety pins, brads and a label.

almost 4

Designer: Jennifer M. Otto

Print journaling onto cardstock, attach eyelets and thread with a jewelry chain. Create the background from patterned paper, cardstock and a photo. Stamp the title and create a tag from an inked number stencil, ribbon and stamped tags.

carnival

Designer: Colleen Rivera

Create the background from painted and inked patterned paper and cardstock. Double mat a photo, stamp the title onto the mat and hang the mat from metal hangers and ribbon. Finish the layout with stamps, ribbon, brads and a staple.

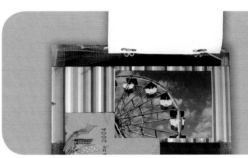

a late night swim

Designer: Michelle Hubbartt

Print part of the title and journaling onto title squares and finish the title with painted metal letters. Attach the title to the page with wire. Create the background from sanded and painted patterned paper and a photo. Embellish the layout with stickers, ribbon, flowers, flip-flops and a metal buckle.

metals

true friend

Designer: Katie Watson

Sand a painted metal bookplate and word. Create the background from patterned paper and cardstock cut into circles. Finish the layout with ink, stamps, ribbon, metal embellishments and a torn vellum quote.

memories of lois

Designer: Katie Watson

Crackle paint a metal bookplate and attach to the background over the bottom part of a tag. Cut a flower shape from cardstock, place under the stripe patterned paper and sand until an image of the flower appears. Create the background from distressed patterned paper and a photo.

happy birthday card

Designer: Wendy Malichio

Attach a bookplate vertically to the card with ribbon. Embellish the card with cardstock, patterned paper, paint, ink, stamps, vellum and metal brads.

electric

Designer: Wendy Malichio

Create the journaling from labels resting on the ledge of a metal bookplate. Create the background from inked patterned paper and cardstock. Mat photos, ink the mats and finish the layout with sanded stickers, ribbon, metal embellishments and a wooden letter.

working with

11 **3-D embellishments**

3-D embellishments have really simplified the scrapbooking and paper crafting process. What used to take hours of inking, cutting, stitching and stamping, now takes just seconds to find the perfect spot to adhere a 3-D embellishment on a project. These embellishments can add just the right finishing touch to create the feel you want for a page. 3-D embellishments are available in a variety of styles and themes and can help you enjoy your pages even more.

3-D embellishments

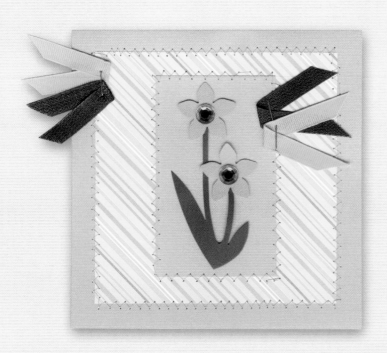

flower card

Designer: Jlyne Hanback

Create the background by zigzag stitching patterned paper and cardstock to a card. Adhere a 3-D embellishment to the cardstock and finish the card with ribbon and staples.

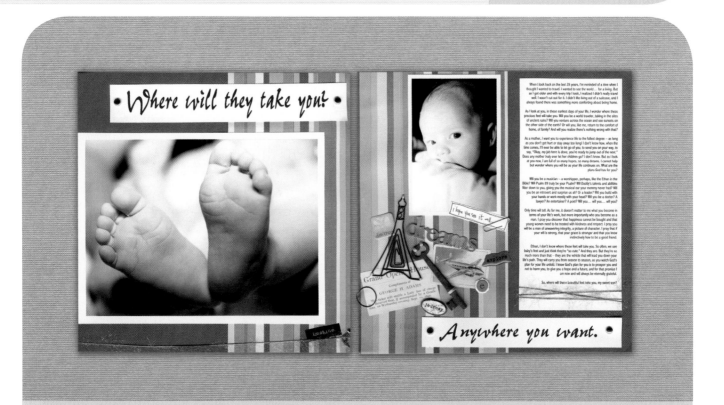

where will they take you?

Designer: Courtney Walsh

Create a collage from metals, 3-D embellishments, tickets, floss, cardstock and stickers. Create the background from patterned paper and cardstock and print the title and journaling onto cardstock. Finish the layout with photos, brads and fiber.

collage

Collages are a great way to add interest to scrapbook pages and projects. Create a collage from different pieces of patterned paper and cardstock for the background of a page or create a collage tag with unique embellishments. A collage is simply a combination of different elements and can be simple or complex. Collages work especially well on cards and tags.

To make a collage, start by gathering different paper and objects. Think about color, scale and intensity. For visual interest it is good to have some light, medium and dark color values, some small, medium and large patterns and some different textures. Look at the objects you have collected to see if they are pleasing. Set the objects out

Ideas for collages:

- Use objects you wouldn't expect to find on a page or card
- Use different scales of paper and objects
- Use different textures

and move them around before adhering them down so you can add or remove objects to make the collage work.

under construction

Designer: Sandra Helder

Mat a photo with torn and inked cardstock and adhere to patterned paper for the background. Embellish the layout with metal letters, stickers and metal charms.

3-D
embellishments

the loveliest
of all card

Designer: Bea Elizalde

Create the background from cardstock and
patterned paper and finish the card with
3-D embellishments.

engaged

Designer: NanC & Company Design

Create the background from
torn patterned paper and
cardstock. Finish the layout
with 3-D embellishments, a
photo and stamps.

joy card

Designer: Bea Elizalde

Embellish a card with rub-ons and a 3-D embellishment.

i love my kitty accordion album

Designer: Susan Stringfellow

Create the cover from inked cardstock, patterned paper, photos, 3-D embellishments, ribbon and metal embellishments. Print photos onto cardstock and sand the cardstock for a soft look. Finish the album by embellishing the rest of the pages.

3-D embellishments

one sweet world

Designer: Felicia Krelwitz

Paint metal accents with acrylic
paint and use for the title and as
the center of flowers. Create the
background from inked patterned
paper, cardstock and a photo.
Embellish the layout with stamps,
ribbon, rub-ons, brads, a sticker
and concho.

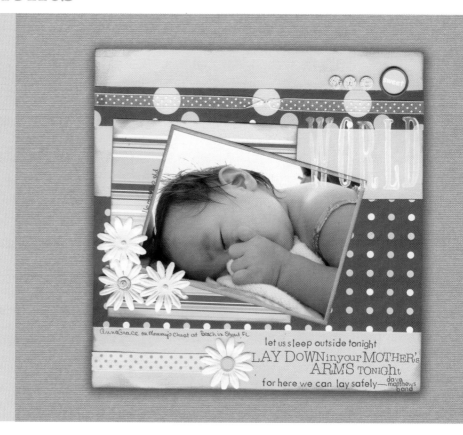

adhesives

Adhesives are the behind the scenes heroes of scrapbookers and paper crafters. They allow us to combine different

elements, paper, embellishments and photos to create our masterpieces. Some elements are more difficult to adhere than

others, so a variety of products are available for our use. Many adhesives are archival safe, but check the packaging to make

sure. The following are types of adhesives our designers have found to be very useful. We hope these will help you with your

hard to adhere objects.

Permanent adhesives

- Square tabs
- Glue pens
- Double sided tape
- Foam and pop dots
- Glue sticks

Re-positionable adhesives

- Hermafix dots
- Spray adhesive (many spray
  adhesives are re-positionable up
  to 24 hours)

Adhesives that add dimension

- Foam dots
- Pop dots
- Diamond glaze

Adhesives for delicate objects

- Xyron machine
- Glue pens

Adhesives for metal and wood

- Pop dots
- Square tabs
- Specialty glue

Adhesives for fabric

- Spray adhesive
- Square tabs

u are my sunshine

Designer: Diana Furey

Create the title from cardstock, patterned paper, tags, stickers and ribbon. Create the background from patterned paper, cardstock and a photo. Finish the layout with ribbon, ink, a flower and metal embellishment.

when my eyes meet your eyes

Designer: Monique Mclean

Create your own 3-D embellishments with patterned paper, flowers, ink and metal letters and adhere them down the side of the page. Create the background from inked patterned paper and cardstock and finish the layout with a photo, rub-ons, ribbon and metal embellishments.

3-D embellishments

aloha card
Designer: Brenda Nakandakari

Adhere patterned paper to a card and finish with 3-D embellishments.

flip-flop card
Designer: Brenda Nakandakari

Attach 3-D embellishments to cardstock and adhere to a card embellished with patterned paper, cardstock and stamps.

majestic view

Designer: Ginger McSwain

Embellish a metal-rimmed tag with sand, seashells, ribbon and a brad. Print journaling onto cardstock and adorn with paint, patterned paper and a 3-D embellishment. Create the background from cardstock, patterned paper, photos and paint.

It seems the older I get the more I find myself appreciating the glorious beauty in nature. We spent 3 wonderful autumn days at Myrtle Beach, S.C. and I think I may have taken as many photos of the ocean, horizon and sealife as I did of the kids! It is truly a refreshing and therapeutic exercise to simply sit and reflect on the beauty in creation that is all around us. -October 11, 2004

perfect summer day

Designer: Tarri Botwinski

Tear, curl, heat emboss with Ultra Thick Embossing Enamel (UTEE) and stitch patterned paper to the background to form waves. Create tags from inked cardstock, stamps and embellishments. Create the background from cardstock, photos, ribbon and rickrack. Finish the layout with stickers, a cardstock title and 3-D embellishment.

3-D embellishments   **170**

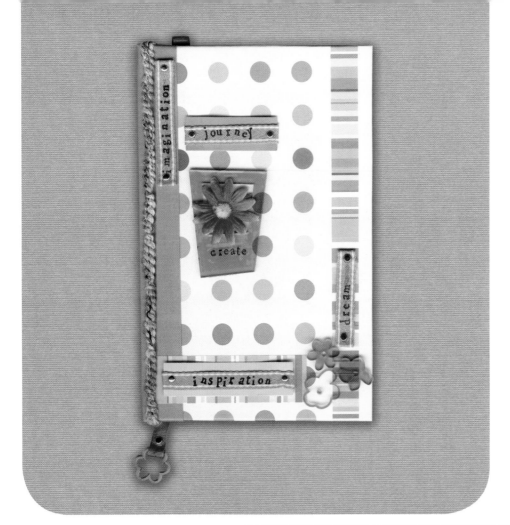

create altered journal

Designer: Susan Stringfellow

Modge podge patterned paper to the cover and binding of a journal. Attach 3-D embellishments and fiber to the cover and create a bookmark from ribbon, a brad and 3-D embellishment.

beautiful flower girl

Designer: Ginger McSwain

Print the title and journaling directly onto cardstock and finish the background with patterned paper, vellum and photos. Embellish the layout with 3-D embellishments, ribbon, metal embellishments and a torn vellum quote.

my new family
accordion frame

Designer: Sam Cousins

Create the backgrounds with inked patterned paper and embellish them with 3-D embellishments and ribbon. Print the title onto a transparency to finish the cover.

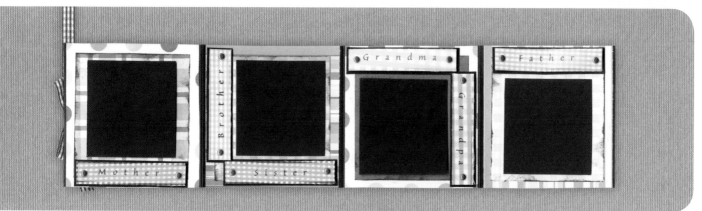

wishes card

Designer: Brenda Nakandakari

Create a card from double-sided cardstock and embellish it with ribbon, cardstock, stamps and 3-D embellishments.

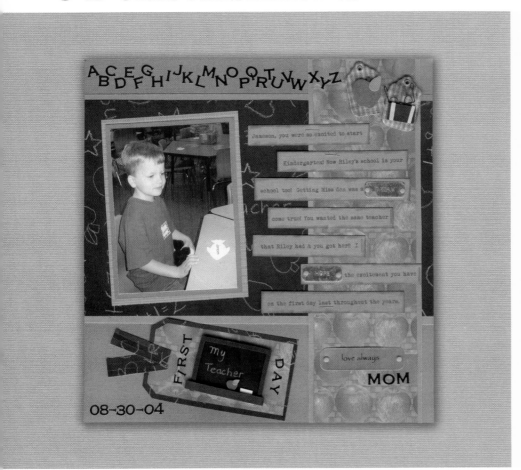

first day

Designer: Tarri Botwinski

Create the background from patterned paper, cardstock, stickers and a photo. Print journaling onto cardstock, ink and attach to the page with staples. Embellish the layout with a tag, 3-D and metal embellishments.

first trip to the beach mini album

Designer: Leah Fung

Create a mini album from chipboard, cardstock and thick wire. Embellish the cover with patterned paper, stitches, 3-D embellishments and a printed tag.

dad tin

Designer: Miranda Isenberg

Paint a CD tin red and embellish
it with painted and stamped
cardboard, metal and cardstock
embellishments and ribbon.

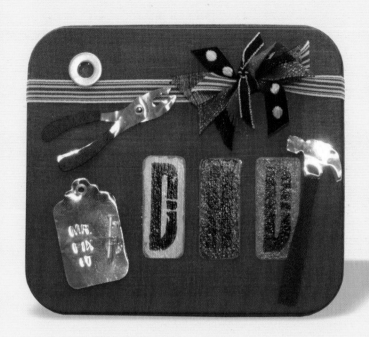

tie card

Designer: Miranda Isenberg

Stamp the title onto vellum
and stitch the vellum to the
background with floss to create
a pocket. Create the background
from patterned paper and
embellish the card with 3-D
embellishments and a tag.

3-D embellishments

gratitude card
Designer: Wendy Malichio

Stamp cardstock, ink and adhere to a card for the background. Embellish the card with printed and inked cardstock, brads, a vellum quote and 3-D embellishment.

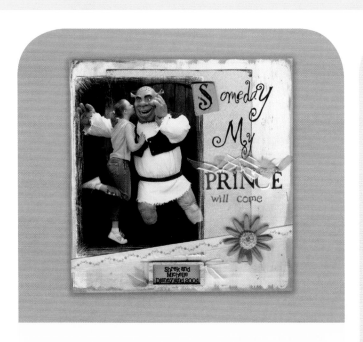

some day my prince will come
Designer: Michelle Hubbartt

Paint chipboard, coat with crystal lacquer, stamp the letter "S" and coat with crystal lacquer again for the beginning of the title. Finish the title with stickers, metal letters and ribbon. Create the background from painted, inked and sanded patterned paper, mesh, fiber paper and a photo. Finish the layout with a frame, transparency, flower and ribbon.

joy tag
Designer: Michelle Gowland

Attach a 3-D embellishment and fibers to a tag.

Step 1

Create a flap in a card by cutting three sides of a rectangle and folding the fourth side back.

Step 2

Attach a transparency behind the opening in the card with brads.

dad card

Designer: NanC & Company Design   ScrapEssentials Jo-Ann

Step 3

Attach 3-D embellishments to the transparency behind the flap and tie the flap closed with ribbon threaded through eyelets. Embellish the card with torn cardstock and letter stickers.

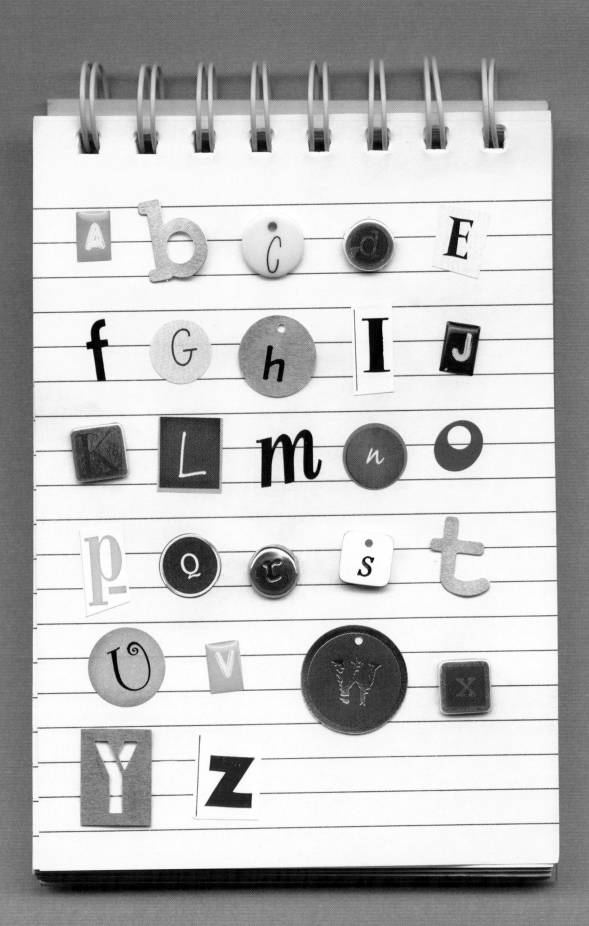

working with
12 alphabets

Okay, let's admit it, we all have a drawer full of letters in some form or another: metal alphabets, letter stickers, stencils, rub-ons, acrylic letters and stamps. We collect them because we love the way they look on our projects, not to mention that they are fast, easy to use and let us avoid handwriting. Finding the perfect monogram letter for a card or the perfect set of metal letters for a title is exhilarating. Notice the different ways our designers use letters in this section and experiment with new ideas of your own.

alphabets

john mayer concert

Designer: Elizabeth Cuzzacrea

Create the title from chipboard letters, stickers and rub-ons. Fill a metal bookplate with stickers, bubbles, fabric labels and a tag. Create the background from patterned paper and cardstock and embellish the layout with journaling tags, ribbon, a distressed card, label and photo.

titles

Have fun with your titles; make them meaningful, witty and full of personality. You will enjoy flipping through your scrapbooks when the pages make you and other viewers laugh. A title gives you an opportunity to sum up your page in a few words. This can be reflective of your feelings, thoughts and actions or simply the event the page is showcasing.

ways to create a title for a page. Determine what look or mood you are trying to create and take clues from your photos and subject. For example, if you are scrapbooking a boy playing with toy blocks, make the title large and blocky. If you are scrapbooking a ballet dance recital, make your letters graceful and delicate.

Ideas for coming up with good titles:

- Brainstorm writing every title that comes to your mind
- Be witty
- Use direct quotes from a family member or friend
- Use the title or lyrics from a poem or song
- Use a quote
- Use scrapbooking title books to get ideas flowing
- Write down good ideas in a notebook to be used later

Ideas for creating titles:

- Print a title onto a transparency and adhere the transparency over your page
- Reverse print a title onto cardstock and cut out with a craft knife
- Cut out letters from a magazine and create a collage title
- Use stickers
- Combine metal letters for a title
- Use templates to cut out letters
- Handwrite your title or have the subject of the page write the title
- Use purchased quotes, titles, tags and headers
- Print a title onto cardstock, trim and mat

How a title looks can determine the mood of a page as much as what the title reads. There are so many different

too sexy
for my hair

Designer: Colleen Rivera

Create the title from letter stickers and metal letters. Create the background from inked patterned paper and cardstock and attach a photo to the page with metal hinges. Embellish the layout with labels, stickers and cards.

rainy day fun

Designer: Cindy Smith

Adhere yellow cardstock to black cardstock for the background and heat emboss the yellow cardstock with Ultra Thick Embossing Enamel (UTEE) for a wet look. Create the title with metal embellishments, letters, wired beads and a crackle painted and stamped wooden tag. Adhere the letters over metal mesh and adhere the metal mesh over black cardstock adhered to the background. Mat photos and adhere to the background. Embellish the layout with a date stamp, metal tag and fiber.

ScrapEssentials Jo-Ann

pumpkin picking

Designer: Rachael Giallongo

Adhere cardstock and a photo to the background. Attach letter stickers along the side of the photo and letter brads below the photo for the title. Finish the layout with ribbon, brads and labels.

ScrapEssentials Jo-Ann

kaylee

Designer: Heather Merical

Create a page on an art canvas for a unique background. Create the background from paint, patterned paper, mesh and a sanded photo. Embellish the layout with printed journaling, sticker letters, fiber, metal embellishments and a card.

laughter is a smile that burst

Designer: Janice Lund

Print journaling onto a transparency and create the title from rub-ons and chipboard letters. Finish the layout with patterned paper, ribbon, and a tag.

improving photos

Great photos make great scrapbook pages! Taking better photos is a guaranteed way to make your pages even better. There are many ways to improve your photos and taking a photography class or reading a book about photography is a great way to start.

Ideas for improving photos:

- Get closer to your subject than you normally would. Take close-up photos of faces, hands, feet, etc. Even when taking photos of a group, get closer to their faces, don't feel like you need to get their feet in the photo

- Focus on lighting. Be aware of sun shining in subjects' faces and squinting. Try to take photos in the shade or use a filler flash so there won't be harsh shadows on your subjects face. When inside try to use natural light as much as possible, making sure the light is enhancing the subject, not behind the subject

- Be aware of the background. Make sure that it is not too distracting and that nothing looks as if it is protruding from the subject's head or limbs. Use the rule of thirds with your backgrounds and scenery photos

- Take candid photos to capture a moment in time and your subject's true personality

- Put subjects at ease with your confidence. Give them ideas on how to pose or give them props to help them feel at ease

winter wish card

Designer: NanC & Company Design

Create the background by adhering two strips of patterned paper onto cardstock. Thread ribbon through a metal word and attach metal embellishments and letter tiles with silver brads.

art

Designer: Colorbok, Inc.

Create a journaling tag by folding a long rectangle of patterned paper in half and then in half again. Handwrite journaling onto the paper, fold and keep closed with buttons and floss. Create the background from patterned paper, cardstock and stitching. Finish the layout with metal letters, paint, nail head eyelets, brads, a photo, image, bookplate and quote.

so happy together card

Designer: Wendy Poling

Cover a library pocket and insert with patterned paper. Print journaling onto cardstock and adhere different letters to the beginning of each sentence. Print the title onto tags, sponge distress ink onto the pocket and insert for continuity and finish the card with a photo, ribbon, mesh and metal embellishments.

ScrapEssentials Jo-Ann

snyders

Designer: NanC & Company Design

Sponge paint metal letters and flowers and adhere to ribbon and fiber. Create the background from cardstock, patterned paper and a photo. Finish the layout with a metal flower, brads, metal words and stamps.

alphabets

he would rather be fishing

Designer: Ginger McSwain

ScrapEssentials JoAnn

Print journaling onto patterned paper and adhere behind a photo attached to the layout with hinges. Create the background from patterned paper, cardstock and a photo. Embellish the layout with a vellum quote, die cuts, metal embellishments and labels.

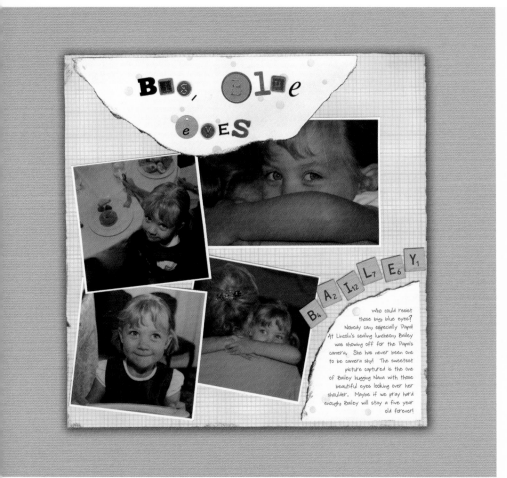

ScrapEssentials JoAnn

big, blue eyes

Designer: NanC & Company Design

Create the title from letter stickers and metal letters. Print journaling onto patterned paper, tear, ink and finish the journaling with scrabble letters. Create the background from inked patterned paper, cardstock and photos.

exploring

Designer: Andrea Ripley

Chalk a tag, attach a vellum quote with eyelets and adorn with fiber. Create the background from patterned paper, cardstock, ribbon and photos. Finish the layout with metal letters, staples, stamps, chalk, brads and a bookplate.

candy door hanger

Designer: Susan Stringfellow

Paint a door hanger and embellish with patterned paper, cardstock, ribbon, rickrack, stickers, metal embellishments and 3-D embellishments.

alphabets

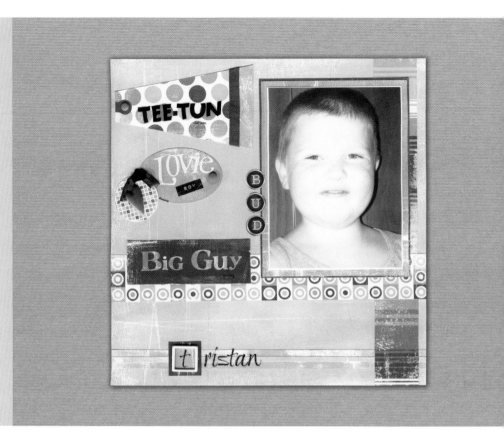

tristan

Designer: Annette Pixley

Create the title and journaling from letter stickers and a label. Create the background from patterned paper and a photo. Embellish the layout with a metal charm, concho and ribbon.

rule of thirds

The rule of thirds is a general design principle that can help you design your pages and projects and take better photos. It is not a rule that always needs to be followed, but when it is used it creates visually pleasing results. If you divide a sheet of paper into a grid of 9 squares, the four corners of the middle square mark the key points of the composition. Put key elements of your composition at these points. Experiment using the rule of thirds on your pages and photos.

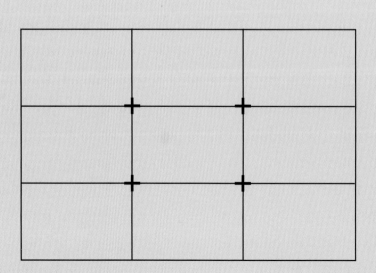

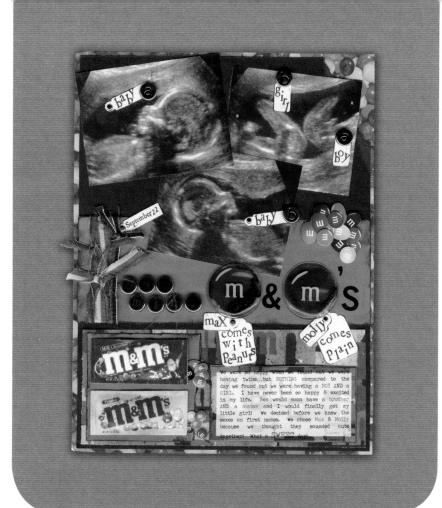

our mini m & m's

Designer: Sam Cousins

Create the title from metal letters, jelly letters and stickers and print journaling onto a transparency. Create the background from patterned paper, cardstock and photos and embellish the layout with stamped tags, ribbon, 3-D embellishments and metal embellishments.

baby girl

Designer: Anna Estrada Davison

Create a tri-fold tag from cardstock and patterned paper. Fill the pockets with letters from mom and dad and embellish the tag with ribbon, quotes, stitching, metal embellishments, stickers and a button. Create the background from patterned paper, cardstock and a photo and embellish the layout with stamps, vellum quotes and metal embellishments.

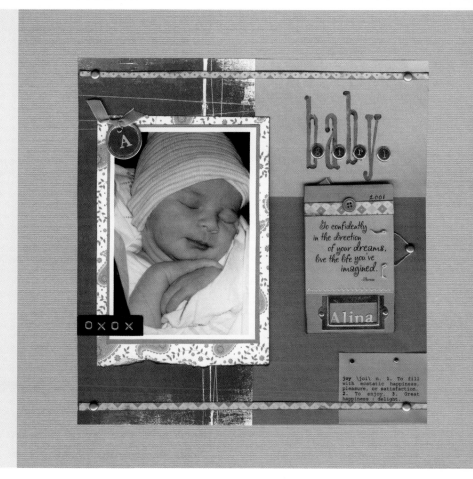

kyle

Designer: Becky DeZarn

Create the title from metal letters and the journaling from labels. Create the background from cardstock and a photo and finish the layout with ribbon, bookplates, brads and a safety pin.

timeless

Designer: Cindy Smith

Create the title with painted metal letters and embellishments. Create the background from stamped cardstock and patterned paper. Distress a photo and definition and embellish the layout with ribbon and a paper clip.

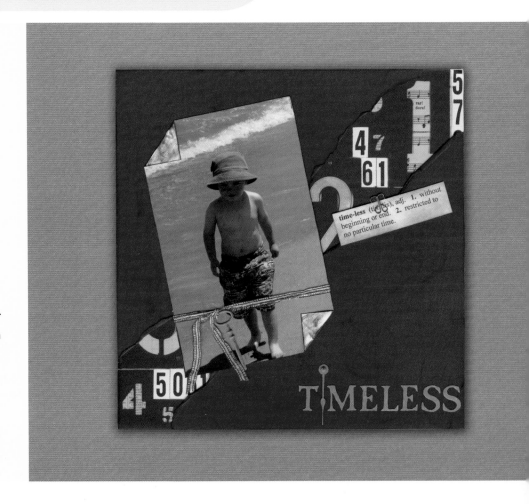

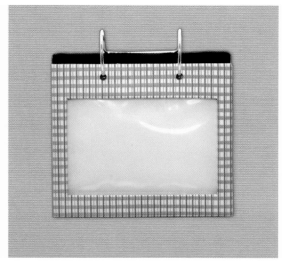

Step 1

Cover the frame of a photo flip album with patterned paper.

Step 2

Adhere cardstock and patterned paper behind the opening of the frame.

christmas advent calendar

Designer: NanC & Company Design

ScrapEssentials JoAnn

Step 3

Embellish the cardstock with rub-ons, handwriting and metal letters. Attach a metal-rimmed tag adorned with letter stickers and ribbon to the cover with a brad.

noel card

Designer: Bea Elizalde

Adhere cardstock and patterned paper to a mini card and adorn with letter brads.

what could be better . . .

Designer: Kristi Mangan

Create the title from letter stickers. Handwrite journaling onto a tag and slide behind a matted photo. Finish the layout with ribbon, staples, tags, brads and a bookplate.

travel

Designer: NanC & Company Design

Paint metal letters and scratch off some of the paint. Create the background from patterned paper, cardstock and a photo. Embellish the layout with cut tiles for photo corners, fiber, a vellum quote, bubble, vellum envelope and metal-rimmed tag.

love tag

Designer: Anna Estrada Davison

Create a tag from patterned paper and embellish it with metal embellishments, stitching, fiber, ink, a vellum quote, sticker and tag.

a wish is a dream your heart makes

Designer: Sherry Laffoon

Create the title from a collage of letter and word embellishments attached to three tags made from patterned paper and cardstock. Create the background from patterned paper, mulberry paper and cardstock. Finish the layout with a photo, sticker, crystal dot and ribbon.

savor the moment

Designer: Susan Weinroth

Stamp the title and print the journaling onto paper, trim and stitch to the layout. Finish the title with metal, wood and acrylic letters. Print words onto fabric, stitch and attach below a photo with safety pins and ribbon. Finish the layout with patterned paper, cardstock, ribbon, leather and metal embellishments and stamps.

sisters
and friends

Designer: Kristi Mangan

Create the background from
patterned paper, cardstock and
a photo. Embellish the layout
with letter stickers, quotes,
ribbon, rickrack, staples, ink
and a metal word.

your smile

Designer: Creative Imaginations

Create the title from patterned
paper and create the background
from cardstock, matted patterned
paper and a photo. Embellish the
layout with photos turns, brads
and ribbon.

project supplies

Key:

AMM	All My Memories
CTMH	Close To My Heart
CI	Creative Imaginations
DCWV	DieCuts With a View
FBTY	Fibers by the Yard
HARS	Hero Arts Rubber Stamps, Inc.
KI	KI Memories
MM	Making Memories
MAMBI	Me & My Big Ideas
MITM	Memories in the Making
PC	Provo Craft
2Peas	Two Peas in a Bucket

CARDSTOCK

2nd birthday
Cardstock: Bazzill
Ribbon: CTMH
Stamps: MM, Purple Onion Designs
Ink: Tsukineko

babe boi
Cardstock: Bazzill
Patterned Paper: Melissa Frances
Tag: Melissa Frances
Eyelet: MM
Ribbon: MM
Ink: Ranger Industries
Fonts: Maiandra, Perpetua

boys and their toys
Cardstock: Bazzill
Patterned Paper: SEI
Punches: EK Success
Stamp: MM, HARS
Ink: Ranger Industries, Tsukineko

holiday card & tag
Cardstock: DCWV
Patterned Paper: 7 Gypsies, The Rusty
Pickle, Karen Foster
Ephemera: TimbuckToo Productions
Rub-ons: Scrapworks, LLC
Metal Embellishments: MM
Paint: MM
Ink: Ranger Industries

if only
Patterned Paper: KI
Die Cuts: KI
Paper Flower: MM
Stickers: Sticker Studio, SEI
Rub-ons: MM
Brads: JoAnn Essentials, Bazzill

jackson
Cardstock: DCWV
Patterned Paper: DCWV
Metal Letters: JoAnn Essentials
Bookplate: JoAnn Essentials
Bubble Alphabet: JoAnn Essentials
Alphabet Brads: JoAnn Essentials
Bubble: JoAnn Essentials

last taste of summer
Cardstock: MITM
Brads: JoAnn Essentials
Tag: JoAnn Essentials
3-D Embellishments: JoAnn Essentials
Fibers: Scrapgoods
Font: Stamp Act, Thinbaby

megan at 8
Cardstock: Chatterbox, Inc.
Brads: JoAnn Essentials
Rub-ons: MM
Metal Number: MM
Stickers: Wordsworth Stamps
Stamps: MoBe' Stamps

miracle
Cardstock: Bazzill
Rub-ons: MM
Paper Flower: MM
Brad: JoAnn Essentials
Paint: Academy Acrylic

our little boy lincoln
Cardstock: DCWV
Patterned Paper: DCWV
Rub-ons: MM
Bubbles: JoAnn Essentials
Button: JoAnn Essentials
Metal Tags: JoAnn Essentials

our song
Patterned Paper: DCWV
Stickers: JoAnn Essentials
Brads: JoAnn Essentials
Conchos: Magic Scraps
Stamps: EK Success, MM
Ink: Tsukineko
Font: Typical Writer, CAC Futura Casual

perfection
Cardstock: Bazzill
Patterned Paper: BasicGrey
Stickers: BasicGrey
Tag: BasicGrey
Ribbon: Offray & Son, Inc.
Photo Turns: MM
Stamps: PSX Design
Ink: Ranger Industries

pumpkin patch
Patterned Paper: DCWV
Stickers: JoAnn Essentials, Bo-Bunny Press
Brads: JoAnn Essentials
Rub-ons: Autumn Leaves
Stamps: EK Success, MM
Ink: Ranger Industries
Font: Typical Writer

puppy love
Cardstock: Bazzill
Bookplate: JoAnn Essentials
Brads: MM
Punch: EK Success
Font: CK Cursive,
Copperplate Gothic Light

so stinkin' adorable
Patterned Paper: BasicGrey
Stickers: MM
Ribbon: Offray & Son, Inc.
Ink: All Night Media

surfin' fun 'n games
Cardstock: Bazzill
Paint: Delta Crafts
Tiles: JoAnn Essentials

VELLUM & TRANSPARENCY

best friends
Cardstock: Bazzill
Patterned Paper: DCWV
Stickers: Bo-Bunny Press
Buttons: Dress It Up!
Brads: JoAnn Essentials
Bookplate: JoAnn Essentials
Ribbon: MM
Floss: DMC
Stamps: Stamp Craft, MM
Ink: Tsukineko
Paints: MM

cheerfulness
Patterned Paper: Arctic Frog
Stickers: Arctic Frog
Ribbon: May Arts, Offray & Son, Inc.,
Adorned Pages
Vellum Quote: JoAnn Essentials
Staples: MM
Ink: Ranger Industries

european vacation
Cardstock: DCWV
Vellum Quote: JoAnn Essentials
Bookplate: JoAnn Essentials
Brads: JoAnn Essentials
Stickers: DCWV

fieldtrip
Patterned Paper: Pebbles Inc.
Ink: Ranger Industries
Hinges: MM
Jump Rings: MM
Mesh: Magenta Rubber Stamps

flowers heal the soul
Cardstock: Bazzill
Patterned Paper: Chatterbox, Inc.
Ribbon Charm: MM

kale & mums
Patterned Paper: DCWV
Stickers: American Craft, Mrs. Grossman
Sticker Quote: EK Success
Ribbon: FBTY, Offray & Son, Inc.

kiss
Patterned Paper: SEI,
Chatterbox, Inc., 7 Gypsies
Acrylic Tile: KI
Brads: CI
Rub-ons: MM
Clip: MM
Photo Corners: MM
Ribbon: MM
Page Pebble: MM
Buckle: MM
Vellum Quote: Deja Views

limbo, limbo, limbo!
Patterned Paper: The Rusty Pickle
3-D Embellishments: Jolee's Boutique
Stamp: Leave Memories

little woolen stockings
Cardstock: Bazzill, Scrap in a Snap
Patterned Paper: Chatterbox, Inc.
Ribbon: Offray & Son, Inc.
Stickers: Chatterbox, Inc.
Bookplate: JoAnn Essentials

Vellum Quote: DCWV
Brads: JoAnn Essentials
Stamps: MM

live in the moment
Patterned Paper: DCWV
Brads: JoAnn Essentials
Vellum Quote: JoAnn Essentials
Metal Tags: JoAnn Essentials
Stamps: MM

me
Cardstock: Bazzill
Patterned Paper: 7 Gypsies, K & Company,
MAMBI, Karen Foster, PC
Transparency: Artistic Expressions
Photo Turns: 7 Gypsies
Vellum Tag: JoAnn Essentials
Metal Letters: JoAnn Essentials
Photo Corners: MM
Stamps: Inkadinkado, Stampabilities
Ink: Ranger Industries, Stampin' Up,
Tsukineko, Postmodern Design

meant to be
Patterned Paper: PC
Transparency: Artistic Expressions
Hinges: MM
Snaps: MM
Word Charm: JoAnn Essentials
Floss: DMC
Ink: Stampin' Up

my time
Cardstock: Bazzill
Patterned Paper: PC
Transparency: K & Company
Stickers: JoAnn Essentials
Stamps: EK Success,
PSX Design, HARS, MM
Charm: A Charming Place
Ribbon: CTMH
Paint: MM
Fonts: American Typewriter, Kayleigh

our family
Cardstock: DCWV
Patterned Paper: MITM
Vellum Quote: JoAnn Essentials
Tags: JoAnn Essentials
Brads: JoAnn Essentials
Button: JoAnn Essentials

sisters
Patterned Paper: Chatterbox, Inc.
Stickers: Chatterbox, Inc.
Tacks: Chatterbox, Inc.
Brads: MM
Tags: MM
Ribbon: SEI, Li'l Davis Designs, 7 Gypsies

tennis
Cardstock: DCWV
Patterned Paper: DCWV
Word Charm: JoAnn Essentials
Word Brad: JoAnn Essentials
Brads: JoAnn Essentials
Metal Letters: JoAnn Essentials

waikiki beach
Patterned Paper: Chatterbox, Inc.
Stickers: CI
Vellum Quote: JoAnn Essentials
Bookplate: JoAnn Essentials
Tacks: Chatterbox, Inc.
Old Postcard: MAMBI

PATTERNED PAPER

baby mobile
Embroidery Hoop
Cardstock: DCWV
Patterned Paper: DCWV
Buttons: JoAnn Essentials
Ribbon: Offray & Son, Inc.

blue eyed beauty
Cardstock: The Rusty Pickle
Patterned Paper: The Rusty Pickle
Fiber: JoAnn Essentials
Eyelets: JoAnn Essentials
Die Cuts: Sizzix
Ink: CTMH

brothers
Cardstock: Bazzill
Patterned Paper: SEI
Ribbon: May Arts
Rub-ons: Autumn Leaves
Tag: Avery
Stamps: MM
Paint: MM

chatty girl
Patterned Paper: BasicGrey
Stickers: BasicGrey
Brads: JoAnn Essentials
Bookplate: JoAnn Essentials
Cardstock Tag: MM
Fabric Saying: MAMBI
Ribbon: May Arts
Stamps: MM
Ink: Ranger Industries

colorful you
Patterned Paper: 7 Gypsies, KI
Leather Flowers: MM
Mesh: MM
Brads: MM
Safety Pins: Li'l Davis Designs
Chipboard Letter: Li'l Davis Designs
Ribbon: May Arts
Acrylic Squares: KI

don't bug me
Patterned Paper: MITM
Punches: EK Success
3-D Embellishments: JoAnn Essentials

eloquent kiss
Cardstock: Bazzill, MM
Pattered Paper: Paper Fever, Inc., SEI
Vellum: SEI
Metal Strip: MM
Rub-ons: MM

experience rome
Cardstock: DCWV
Patterned Paper: MITM
Fiber: JoAnn Essentials
Brads: JoAnn Essentials
Tag: JoAnn Essentials
Bubbles: JoAnn Essentials
Alphabet Brads: JoAnn Essentials
Bookplate: JoAnn Essentials
Stamps: MM

friendship
Cardstock: DCWV
Patterned Paper: DCWV
Vellum Quote: DCWV
Brads: MM
Tacks: Chatterbox, Inc.
Ink: Stampin' Up, Altered Pages

happy
Patterned Paper: SEI
Rub-ons: SEI
Brads: MM
Photo Turns: SEI

happy birthday tag
Patterned Paper: DCWV
Bookplate: JoAnn Essentials
Conchos: JoAnn Essentials
Brads: JoAnn Essentials
3-D Embellishment: JoAnn Essentials
Stickers: DCWV
Ink: Ranger Industries

happy family
Cardstock: Bazzill
Patterned Paper: KI
Stickers: Paperfever, Inc.
Paper Flowers: MM
Brads: MM
Stencil Letter: JoAnn Essentials
Bookplate: JoAnn Essentials
Ribbon: Offray & Son, Inc.

happy holidays card
Patterned Paper: DCWV
Overlay: DCWV
Metal Charms: MM
Metal Words: MM
Ribbon: Offray & Son, Inc.

hi card
Canning Lid
Cardstock: KI, Bazzill
Patterned Paper: Paperfever, Inc.
Tiles: JoAnn Essentials
Metal Charm: JoAnn Essentials
Ribbon: Lifetime Moments
Rub-ons: MM
Paint: MM

it's about time
Cardstock: Bazzill, Pebbles, Inc.
Patterned Paper: Carolee's Creations,
Outdoors & More
Frame: Forget Me Not Designs
Wood Flower: Li'l Davis Designs
Alphabet Charms: Li'l Davis Designs
Stickers: K & Company, Mustard Moon
Paper Co..
Ribbon: May Arts
Stamps: MM, CTMH
Ink: Ranger Industries
Font: 2 Peas Magic Forest

just a little note
CD Tin
Bookplate: JoAnn Essentials
Brads: JoAnn Essentials
Bubbles: JoAnn Essentials
Tag: JoAnn Essentials

life is groovy
Cardstock: Bazzill
Patterned Paper: SEI
Stickers: SEI
Rub-ons: SEI
Buttons: SEI
Ribbon: SEI
Stamp: MM
Ink: Stampin' Up

love bag
Cardstock: DCWV
Patterned Paper: DCWV
3-D Embellishment: JoAnn Essentials

love card
Cardstock: Stampin' Up
Patterned Paper: KI, 7 Gypsies
Die Cut: KI
Acrylic Word: KI
Ribbon: Offray & Son, Inc.
Ink: Ranger Industries

loved
Patterned Paper: KI, Chatterbox, Inc., SEI
Ribbon: SEI
Stickers: MM, SEI, AMM
Tacks: Chatterbox, Inc.
Rivets: Chatterbox, Inc.
Tag: MM
Brads: MM
Ribbon Slide: Li'l Davis Designs

merry christmas card
Cardstock: DCWV
Patterned Paper: DCWV

moments of solitude
Cardstock: DCWV
Patterned Paper: KI
Rub-ons: MM
Stamps: HARS
Ink: Tsukineko

quinn
Cardstock: DCWV
Patterned Paper: DCWV
Stickers: DCWV
Metal Stickers: JoAnn Essentials
Brads: JoAnn Essentials
Tags: JoAnn Essentials
Floss: DMC
Ink: ColorBox

smile
Patterned Paper: Miss Elizabeth's
Cardstock Tags: DCWV
Metal Letters: JoAnn Essentials
Stamps: PSX Design
Ink: ColorBox

sour
Patterned Paper: KI, American Crafts
Stickers: Doodlebug Designs Inc.,
American Crafts
Brads: JoAnn Essentials
Bookplate: MM

**the ups & downs
of anna grace**
Patterned Paper: BasicGrey
Stickers: MM, BasicGrey
Brads: MM
Ribbon: ScrapAddict
Stamps: MM
Ink: Tsukineko

travel abroad
Cardstock: DCWV
Patterned Paper: MITM
Stickers: JoAnn Essentials
Tag: JoAnn Essentials
Fibers: JoAnn Essentials
Vellum Quote: JoAnn Essentials
Brads: JoAnn Essentials
Stamps: MM

treasure
Cardstock: The Paper Company
Rivets: Chatterbox, Inc.
Wood Frame: Li'l Davis Designs
Stamp: MM
Ink: Ranger Industries

vacation mode
Cardstock: Bazzill
Patterned Paper: NRN Designs,
BasicGrey, KI
Jigsaw Letters: MM
Rub-ons: MM
Bookplate: MM
Ribbon: MM, May Arts
Stamps: PSX Design
Ink: Ranger Industries
Brads: Bazzill
Font: 2 Peas Roxie

water lily
Cardstock: Bazzill
Patterned Paper: KI
Stickers: KI, Pebbles, Inc.
Paper Flowers: MM
Brads: Scrapworks, LLC
Ink: Ranger Industries

who are you?
Patterned Paper: DCWV, Sweetwater
Brads: JoAnn Essentials
Metal Word: JoAnn Essentials
Ribbon: Offray & Son, Inc., FBTY
Stamps: MM
Tag: MM
Font: 2 Peas Blonde and Ding Bats

you are mine
Cardstock: National Cardstock
Patterned Paper: The Paper Loft
Stickers: Wordsworth Stamps
Metal Word: MM
Brads: MM
Bookplate: MM
Paper Flower: MM
Photo Turns: MM
Ribbon: May Arts
Stamps: MM
Paint: MM
Ink: Ranger Industries

BRADS & EYELETS

a summer of leaps
Patterned Paper: Arctic Frog
Stickers: Arctic Frog
Twistel: MM
Font: AceBingham SH

a trip to remember album
Playing Cards
Stickers: CI, MM
Stamps: Ma Vinci's Reliquary
Magic Mesh: MM
Waxy Flax: Scrapworks, LLC
Paint: Delta Crafts

celebrate good times
Patterned Paper: BasicGrey
Stickers: BasicGrey
Brads: MM
Eyelets: MM
Stamps: MM
Envelope Template: Deluxe Designs
Ink: Stampin' Up

christmas tree tag
Cardstock: DCWV
Patterned Paper: DCWV
Metal Words: JoAnn Essentials
Brads: JoAnn Essentials
Ribbon: Offray & Son, Inc.
Metal Star: MM

congratulations gift bag
Cardstock: DCWV
Patterned Paper: DCWV
Brads: JoAnn Essentials
Stickers: DCWV
Ribbon: Offray & Son, Inc.

forever card
Patterned Paper: Colorbok, Inc.
Bookplate: JoAnn Essentials
Woven Label: JoAnn Essentials
Brads: JoAnn Essentials
Eyelets: JoAnn Essentials
Vellum Quote: JoAnn Essentials
Jump Rings: Darice
Ribbon: Offray & Son, Inc.

giggle
Cardstock: Bazzill
Stickers: MM
Eyelets: MM
Chalks: EK Success
Ribbon: Offray & Son, Inc.
Floss: DMC

gingerbread boy card
Cardstock: DCWV
Patterned Paper: DCWV
3-D Embellishment: JoAnn Essentials
Sticker: DCWV

gingerbread girl card
Cardstock: DCWV
Patterned Paper: DCWV
3-D Embellishment: JoAnn Essentials
Sticker: DCWV

jolly
Cardstock: DCWV
Patterned Paper: DCWV
Word Eyelets: JoAnn Essentials
Alphabet Clip: JoAnn Essentials
Fibers: FBTY
Ribbon: Wrights Ribbon Accents
Brads: JoAnn Essentials
Stamps: HARS, MM
Ink: Tsukineko, Stampin' Up
Fonts: Stencil BT, P22 Oh Lay,
Americana BT

my favorite things about fall
Cardstock: The Paper Company
Patterned Paper: MM
Tag: Paperbilities
Stickers: Sticko
Conchos: K & Company
Staples: MM
Floss: DMC
Brads: MM
Stamps: MM, PSX Design

rebel
Patterned Paper: The Paper Loft
Chalk Ink: ColorBox
Font: P22 Garamouche

red, white & blue
Cardstock: DCWV
Patterned Paper: DCWV
Stickers: DCWV
3-D Embellishments: JoAnn Essentials
Bookplate: JoAnn Essentials
Tags: JoAnn Essentials
Brads: JoAnn Essentials
Chalk: Craf-T Products
Stamps: MM
Ink: CTMH

savor
Cardstock: DCWV
Patterned Paper: DCWV
Brads: JoAnn Essentials
Metal Work: JoAnn Essentials
Stickers: DCWV
Ink: ColorBox

FLOSS & WIRE

family is forever
Cardstock: Bazzill
Linen Alphabet: Li'l Davis Designs
Die Cuts: Daisy D's Paper Company, Sizzix
Paper Flower: MM
Walnut Ink: Magic Scraps
Brads: JoAnn Essentials
Ribbon: Offray & Son, Inc.
Chalk Pad: Inkadinkado

forever
Cardstock: DCWV
Patterned Paper: DCWV
Bookplates: JoAnn Essentials
Rub-ons: MM
Brad: JoAnn Essentials
Stamps: MM

just add water
Patterned Paper: Li'l Davis Designs
Stickers: Wordsworth Stamps
Beads: CI

learn
Patterned Paper: Chatterbox, Inc., Anna
Griffin, CI, The Rusty Pickle
Metal Tags: JoAnn Essentials
Bookplate: JoAnn Essentials
Ribbon: Li'l Davis Designs,
Offray & Son, Inc.
Ink: Ranger Industries
Paint: American Crafts

miracle of christmas magnet
Cardboard Coaster
Cardstock: DCWV
Patterned Paper: DCWV
Metal Charms: JoAnn Essentials
Word Eyelet: JoAnn Essentials
Alphabet Brads: JoAnn Essentials
Wire: Artistic Wire Ltd.
Beads: Altered Pages
Stamps: HARS, MM

nana's keepsake box
Fabric: JoAnn Fabric & Crafts
Ribbon: DCWV
Floss: MM
Brad: JoAnn Essentials

reflections of you
Cardstock: DCWV
Patterned Paper: BasicGrey
Rub-ons: CI
Sticker: CI
Brads: MM
Monogram Letter: JoAnn Fabric & Crafts

safe in brothers arms
Patterned Paper: Daisy D's Paper
Company
Twill Tape: JoAnn Fabric & Crafts
Metal Clips: 7 Gypsies
Eyelets: MM
Staples: MM
Jump Rings: MM
Rub-ons: CI
Ink: Ranger Industries

silly
Cardstock: DCWV
Patterned Paper: DCWV
Buttons: DCWV
Vellum Quote: JoAnn Essentials

snowman card
Card: DCWV
Brads: JoAnn Essentials

thankful
Cardstock: DCWV
Patterned Paper: DCWV
Vellum Quote: DCWV
Stickers: DCWV
3-D Embellishments: JoAnn Essentials
Brad: JoAnn Essentials
Floss: DMC
Punch: Marvy Uchida

the fruits of our labor
Patterned Paper: BasicGrey
Vellum: Autumn Leaves
Rub-ons: MM
Pocket Template: Deluxe Designs
Ribbon: May Arts
Ink: Ranger Industries, Tsukineko
Chalk: Pebbles Inc.

the perfect day
Patterned Paper: MM
Bookplate: JoAnn Essentials
Ribbon: JoAnn Fabric & Crafts
Fiber: Scrapworks, LLC
Brads: MM, CI
Paper Flowers: MM
Safety Pin: MM
Stamp: MM
Ink: Ranger Industries

unconditional love
Cardstock: Bazzill
Patterned Paper: BasicGrey
Bookplate: Li'l Davis Designs
Wire Connector: 7 Gypsies
Metal Frame: MM
Rub-ons: MM
Brads: MM
Stamps: MM
Ink: Ranger Industries

warm wishes card
Brads: JoAnn Essentials
Gemstones: JoAnn Essentials
Floss: DMC

FIBER, RIBBON & FABRIC

35 years
Cardstock: MM
Patterned Paper: Karen Foster
Stickers: EK Success
Safety Pin: The Happy Hammer
Vellum Tag: MM
Stamp: MM, Plaid Enterprises, Inc.

always
Patterned Paper: Chatterbox, Inc.,
7 Gypsies
Stickers: Pebbles, Inc., Wordsworth Stamps,
MAMBI
Photo Turns: 7 Gypsies
Ribbon: May Arts

ballet frame
Frame
3-D Embellishments: JoAnn Essentials
Ribbon: Offray & Son, Inc.

body art
Patterned Paper: BasicGrey, Pebbles, Inc.
Tags: BasicGrey
Stickers: BasicGrey
Eyelets: MM
Rub-ons: MM
Stencil: Autumn Leaves
Hemp Fabric: Artistic Scrapper
Bookplate: Li'l Davis Designs
Walnut Ink: Magic Scraps

can i keep him
Patterned Paper: 7 Gypsies, Daisy D's
Paper Company, The Rusty Pickle
Ribbon: Offray & Son, Inc.
Stickers: Phrase Café, Bo-Bunny Press
Stamps: All Night Media
Paint: Plaid Enterprises, Inc.
Font: Mandingo

christmas card
Patterned Paper: DMD Industries
Ribbon: MM
Metal Charm: MM
Brads: JoAnn Essentials, MM
Ribbon Slide: MM
Tags: DMD Industries

collage necklace
Frame: JoAnn Essentials
Charm: Quest Inc.
Necklace End: Darice
Spring Ring: Darice

dear santa door hanger
Chipboard
Patterned Paper: DCWV
Ribbon: FBTY
Stickers: DCWV, David Walker
Metal Letters: JoAnn Essentials

escape pocket book
Cardstock: Bazzill
Patterned Paper: MAMBI
Fabric Paper: MAMBI
Rub-ons: MAMBI

family time
Patterned Paper: K & Company, BasicGrey
Tag: JoAnn Essentials
Word Brads: JoAnn Essentials
Sticker: DCWV
Stamp: Magenta Rubber Stamps
Rivets: Marcella by Kay
Ink: Ranger Industries
Font: 2 Peas RagTag

from paradise
Patterned Paper: MAMBI
Stickers: MAMBI
Ribbon: MAMBI
Paper Embellishments: MAMBI
Vintage Threads: MAMBI
Ephemera: MAMBI
Ink: Ranger Industries

goofey's kitchen
Patterned Paper: BasicGrey
Tag: BasicGrey
Stickers: BasicGrey, PC
Ribbon: Offray & Son, Inc.
Bottle Caps: Li'l Davis Designs
Metal Clip: MM
Font: 2 Peas Jack Frost

grandma mini album
Mini Album: Paperbilities
Cardstock: DCWV
Bookplate: JoAnn Essentials
Brads: JoAnn Essentials
Stickers: DCWV, JoAnn Essentials
Page Pebbles: CI
Metal Embellishments: JoAnn Essentials
Ribbon: JoAnn Fabric & Crafts, Offray &
Son, Inc.
Vellum Quotes: JoAnn Essentials
Font: Alder, Bernie, 2 Peas Brainless, 2 Peas
Sleigh Ride, P22 Garamouche

halloween tag
Fabric Saying: MAMBI
Ribbon: Offray & Son, Inc.
Gauze: Johnson & Johnson
Bubble: CI
Stamp: StampDiva
Brads: MM
Metal Clip: 7 Gypsies
Ink: ColorBox, Stampin' Up

let it snow card
Patterned Paper: DCWV
Overlay: DCWV
Vellum Quote: DCWV
Metal Charms: MM
Ribbon: Offray & Son, Inc.
Fiber: FBTY

love
Patterned Paper: Autumn Leaves,
Chatterbox, Inc., American Crafts, KI
Letters: My Mind's Eye, Inc.
Brads: JoAnn Essentials
Buttons: American Crafts, Chatterbox, Inc.
Photo Clip: 7 Gypsies
Font: Ameritype

miah clipboard
Patterned Paper: DCWV
3-D Embellishment: JoAnn Essentials
Bookplate: JoAnn Essentials
Stickers: DCWV
Rub-ons: Studio K, K & Company
Ribbon: May Arts, MM, K & Company
Buttons: JoAnn Fabric & Crafts
Paint: Americana
Modge Podge: Plaid Enterprises, Inc.
Stamps: MM

my little angel
Cardstock: Bazzill
Patterned Paper: Daisy D's Paper
Company
Bookplate: MM
Paper Flowers: MM
Rub-ons: MM

our little man tag book
Cardstock: DCWV
Patterned Paper: DCWV
Stickers: DCWV
Rub-ons: MM
Fiber: JoAnn Essentials
Vellum Quotes: DCWV

panther
Cardstock: Bazzill
Ribbon: May Arts
Rub-ons: Craf-T Products
Leather Frame: MM
Stickers: American Crafts

pigtails
Cardstock: Bazzill
Patterned Paper: MAMBI, Chatterbox, Inc.
Brads: The Happy Hammer
Tag: DMD Industries
Snap: MM
Ribbon: Offray & Son, Inc.
Ink: Ranger Industries
Font: Angelina

precious
Cardstock: Bazzill
Patterned Paper: 7 Gypsies,
Autumn Leaves, Sweetwater
Stencil: Autumn Leaves
Ribbon: MM
Paper Flowers: MM
Brads: MM
Font: Chatterbox, Inc. Trumpet

regan
Cardstock: Bazzill
Patterned Paper: Chatterbox, Inc.
Rub-ons: MM
Metal Phrase: MM
Stamp: MM
Ink: Stampin' Up

sewing purse
Measuring Tape: JoAnn Fabric & Crafts
Ribbon: JoAnn Fabric & Crafts
Fabric: JoAnn Fabric & Crafts

**sunshine, freedom
and a little flower**
Cardstock: Bazzill
Patterned Paper: BasicGrey
Flower: ScrapAddict
Brad: MM
Fabric: JoAnn Fabric & Crafts

swing
Patterned Paper: BasicGrey
Ribbon: FBTY
Ink: Tsukineko
Fonts: 2 Peas Stop Sign

under the tuscan sun
Patterned Paper: BasicGrey
Tag: MM
Metal Clip: MM
Ribbon: Offray & Son, Inc.
Font: Vivaldi

STICKERS & STAMPS

2ⁿᵈ grade
Cardstock: Bazzill
Stickers: JoAnn Essentials, DCWV
Metal Tag: MM
Ribbon: Offray & Son, Inc.
Paint: Delta Crafts

a boy and his teddy bear
Cardstock: Westrim Crafts
Patterned Paper: MM, Chatterbox, Inc.
Stickers: Colorbok, Inc.
Photo Corners: MM
Buttons: Westrim Crafts
Font: LB Bonus Marci

**a thing of beauty
file folder card**
Patterned Paper: DCWV
Vellum Quote: JoAnn Essentials
Alphabet Tag: JoAnn Essentials
Stickers: JoAnn Essentials, DCWV
Brad: JoAnn Essentials
Ribbon: MM
Safety Pin: MM
Paper Flower: MM
Ink: Ranger Industries

address book
Heavy Craft Paper
Patterned Paper: Colorbok, Inc.
Bookplate: JoAnn Essentials
Eyelets: JoAnn Essentials

adios card
Cardstock: DCWV
Patterned Paper: DCWV
Stickers: DCWV
Brads: JoAnn Essentials

all about me mini album
Cardstock: MM, Bazzill
Patterned Paper: DCWV, MM
Stickers: DCWV, CI
Vellum Tag: JoAnn Essentials
Brad: JoAnn Essentials
3-D Embellishments: JoAnn Essentials
Ribbon: Offray & Son, Inc.
Bookplate: JoAnn Essentials
Stamps: MM
Paint: Delta Crafts
Ink: Tsukineko

all these things and more
Cardstock: Bazzill
Patterned Paper: Li'l Davis Designs
Bottle Caps: Li'l Davis Designs
Bookplate: Li'l Davis Designs
Stamps: Li'l Davis Designs

amelia & mommy
Patterned Paper: BasicGrey
Tag: BasicGrey
Stencil: Chatterbox, Inc.
Ribbon: MM
Rub-ons: MM
Stamps: MM
Paint: MM
Font: Another Typewriter

back to school tag
Cardstock: Deluxe Designs
Stickers: JoAnn Essentials
Epoxy Sticker: CI
Alphabet Bubble: JoAnn Essentials
Rub-ons: MM
Ink: ColorBox

beach wedding
Cardstock: Bazzill
Patterned Paper: BasicGrey
Stickers: KI
Metal Sticker: AMM
Rub-ons: MM
Fibers: FBTY
Twist Tie: Pebbles, Inc.
Ink: ColorBox

christmas joy
Patterned Paper: DCWV
Stickers: JoAnn Essentials
Fiber: Great Balls of Fiber

creature specs
Cardstock: Bazzill
Patterned Paper: SEI
Cardstock Tab: SEI
Stickers: SEI, KI, Design Originals, Li'l Davis
Designs
Ribbon: May Arts
Stamps: The Rusty Pickle, Image Tree
Ink: Ranger Industries

dancing girl
Cardstock: Bazzill
Patterned Paper: DCWV
Stickers: DCWV
Ribbon: Offray & Son, Inc.
Bow: Queen & Co.
Bookplate: JoAnn Essentials
Brads: JoAnn Essentials
Stamps: MM
Paint: MM
Font: Copperplate Gothic

fear factor
Cardstock: Bazzill
Pattered Paper: KI
Snaps: MM
Tag: MM
Paint: MM
Stamps: MM
Ribbon: FBTY
Pen: CTMH
Alphabet Stencils: Scrapworks, LLC

halloween 2003
Cardstock: DCWV
Patterned Paper: DCWV
Stickers: JoAnn Essentials, DCWV
Fibers: JoAnn Essentials
Ink: Tsukineko

**holiday wishes tin & cd
ornaments**
Patterned Paper: Top Line Creations
Stickers: JoAnn Essentials

**how granddads
survive**
Cardstock: Bazzill
Patterned Paper: Arctic Frog
Stickers: KI, Arctic Frog
Mailbox Letters: MM

how?
Cardstock: Bazzill
Patterned Paper: BasicGrey
Tag: Li'l Davis Designs
Rub-ons: MM, Autumn Leaves,
Scrapworks, LLC
Stamps: The Rusty Pickle, MM
Ink: Ranger Industries

legend of a grandpa
Cardstock: Bazzill
Patterned Paper: K & Company
Stickers: Rebecca Sower
Bookplate: JoAnn Essentials
Eyelets: MM
Metal Mesh: MM
Screw Snaps: MM
Fonts: CK Becky Higgins, Typeset,
Vintage Typewriter

little boy card
Cardstock: DCWV
Patterned Paper: DCWV
Stickers: DCWV
Brads: JoAnn Essentials

little girl
Cardstock: Bazzill
Pattered Paper: Melissa Frances
Cardstock Tab: Melissa Frances
Flowers: MM
Ribbons: May Arts, Impress Rubber Stamps
Hinges: MM
Brads: Chatterbox, Inc., MM
Rub-ons: MM
Stamps: Rubber Stampede, MM
Ink: Ranger Industries

pure joy
Cardstock: Bazzill
Patterned Paper: K & Company
Ribbon Charm: MM
Ribbon: CTMH

Stamps: MM
Ink: Ranger Industries
Paint: MM

real love
Cardstock: Bazzill
Patterned Paper: BasicGrey
Brads: MM
Stamps: Magenta Rubber Stamps, MM,
Wordsworth Stamps
Ink: Tsukineko
Paint: MM

school time
Patterned Paper: AMM,
Karen Foster Design
Stickers: JoAnn Essentials, O'Scrap
Tag: Rebecca Sower
Rub-ons: Autumn Leaves
Ribbon: MM
Learn Charm: Darice
Date Stamp: MM
Ink: Rubber Stampede

seasons greetings card
Patterned Paper: DCWV
Stickers: JoAnn Essentials
Brads: JoAnn Essentials
3-D Embellishments: JoAnn Essentials
Metal Embellishments: JoAnn Essentials

**sweet summer
beach babe**
Patterned Paper: BasicGrey
Stickers: Sweetwater, CI
Rub-ons: MM
Ribbon: May Arts
Paint: MM
Ink: Tsukineko

the boogie board
Cardstock: DCWV, National Cardstock
Patterned Paper: The Rusty Pickle
Punch: Marvy Uchida
Stamps: Post Modern Design
Ink: Ranger Industries
Font: Batik Regular

time capsule
Cardstock: DCWV
Patterned Paper: DCWV
Stickers: JoAnn Essentials
Stamps: MM
Ribbon: DCWV

trick or treat tag
Patterned Paper: DCWV
Stickers: DCWV, Mrs. Grossman's
Staples: MM
Brads: JoAnn Essentials
Metal Word: JoAnn Essentials
Ribbon: JoAnn Fabric & Crafts
Stamps: MM
Tag & Envelope Template: MM

ENVELOPES & TAGS

1ˢᵗ cream cone
Cork: LazerLetterz
Stickers: MM
Stamps: MM
Ribbon: Maya Road

are we there yet? tag
Cardstock: Bazzill
Patterned Paper: Paper Love Designs
Rub-ons: MM
Brad: MM
Paper Flower: MM
Ribbon: SEI, MM, Li'l Davis Designs
Ink: Ranger Industries

aubrey
Patterned Paper: MAMBI
3-D Embellishments: MAMBI
Rub-ons: MAMBI
Stickers: MAMBI

autumn tag
Cardstock: Bazzill
Patterned Paper: Scenic Route Paper Company
Ribbon: Offray & Son, Inc.
Brad: Adorned Pages
Stickers: MM
Index Tab: Autumn Leaves
Ink: Ranger Industries

brothers
Patterned Paper: AMM
Stickers: Karen Foster, DCWV
Tags: JoAnn Essentials
Stencil: Autumn Leaves
Metal Bars: Karen Foster
Twine: Darice
Stamps: Image Tree

butte, montana
Patterned Paper: KI, Chatterbox, Inc.
Vellum Envelope: JoAnn Essentials
Tag: JoAnn Essentials
Frame: My Mind's Eye, Inc.
Paper Button: My Mind's Eye, Inc.
Stickers: Chatterbox, Inc.
Ribbon: Offray & Son, Inc.
Vellum Quote: DCWV
Stamps: MM
Ink: ColorBox

canada tag
Tags: River City Rubber Works, JoAnn Essentials
3-D Embellishments: JoAnn Essentials
Stickers: Rebecca Sower, Sticker Studio, The Paper Loft, CI
Brad: MM
Safety Pin: MM
Stamps: Image Tree, MM

candy crazy
Patterned Paper: The Rusty Pickle
Stickers: MAMBI
Alphabet: Foofala
Ribbon: May Arts
Label: MM
Ink: Ranger Industries

concerts cd case book
CD Jewel Case and CD
Patterned Paper: Colorbok, Inc.
3-D Embellishments: JoAnn Essentials
Metal Alphabets: JoAnn Essentials
Word Stick Pin: JoAnn Essentials
Vellum Envelopes: JoAnn Essentials

dorm life
Patterned Paper: Chatterbox, Inc.
Stickers: Sticker Studio, Sonnets
Brads: The Happy Hammer, JoAnn Essentials
Rub-ons: MM
Tags: Chatterbox, Inc.
Font: CaslonNo504D

for you tag
Cardstock: Bazzill
Patterned Paper: DCWV
Vellum Envelope: JoAnn Essentials
Tile: JoAnn Essentials
Ribbon: Lifetime Moments
Stamps: Image Tree

gift card envelope
Cardstock: DCWV
Patterned Paper: DCWV
Tags: JoAnn Essentials
Eyelet: JoAnn Essentials
Brads: JoAnn Essentials
Vellum Quote: JoAnn Essentials
Metal Charm: JoAnn Essentials
Fiber: JoAnn Essentials
Ribbon: Offray & Son, Inc.

girlish charm
Patterned Paper: MM, BasicGrey
Bubble Words: CI
Tag: Deluxe Designs
Ribbon: May Arts
Buckle: 7 Gypsies

grandpa
Patterned Paper: The Paper Loft, Karen Foster
Tags: JoAnn Essentials
Vellum Quote: JoAnn Essentials
Metal Words: JoAnn Essentials
Brads: JoAnn Essentials
Fiber: JoAnn Essentials
Rub-ons: MM
Stamps: PSX Design, Ranger Industries

gratitude tag
Cardstock: Bazzill
Patterned Paper: K & Company
Definition: MM
Hinges: MM
Brads: Adorned Pages
Stickers: Pebbles, Inc.
Fibers: FBTY

in the blink of an eye
Patterned Paper: BasicGrey
Tag: BasicGrey
Metal Plaques: MM
Leather Frame: MM
Rub-ons: MM
Bookplate: MM
Metal Phrase: MM
Metal Alphabet: MM
Brads: Boxer Scrapbooks
Ribbon: May Arts
Watch Charm: With Charm
Rickrack: Wrights Ribbon Accents
Fabric: K & Company
Stickers: K & Company, Just My Type
Stamp: MM
Paint: Plaid Enterprises, Inc.

just relax
Cardstock: Bazzill
Patterned Paper: KI
Die Cuts: KI
Stickers: KI
File Folder: The Rusty Pickle
Photo Corners: MM
Stamps: MM
Ink: ColorBox, Tsukineko

kimble & kara frame
Cardstock: DCWV
Patterned Paper: DCWV
Vellum Envelopes: JoAnn Essentials
Tags: JoAnn Essentials
Stickers: DCWV

little champion
Patterned Paper: DCWV
Stickers: JoAnn Essentials
Metal Word: JoAnn Essentials
Tag: JoAnn Essentials
Ribbon: MM
Safety Pin: MM
Ink: Ranger Industries
Fonts: LB Loni, Arial, Times New Roman, P22 Garamouche

live
Patterned Paper: BasicGrey
Tag: BasicGrey
Rub-ons: MM
Fibers: FBTY

loved 4 ever
Patterned Paper: BasicGrey, Anna Griffin
Paper Flowers: MM
Brads: MM
Stickers: Chatterbox, Inc., Art Warehouse
Acrylic Flower: KI
Transparency: 7 Gypsies
Bubble Alphabet: K & Company

magic happens
Patterned Paper: Paper Love Design
Vellum Quote: DCWV
Metal Letters: JoAnn Essentials
Conchos: JoAnn Essentials
Tag: My Mind's Eye, Inc., 7 Gypsies
Ribbon: May Arts
Brads: Stampin' Up
Fabric Corners: MM
Paint: MM

accordion tag book
Cardstock: DCWV
Patterned Paper: DCWV
Tag Die Cut: Sizzix
Mickey Tag: Eyelet Outlet
Brads: JoAnn Essentials
Metal Letters: ScrapYard 329
Fibers: FBTY
Metal Clip: MM
Stamps: HARS, Rubber Stamp Ave.
Ink: Stampin' Up
Font: Disney Simple

miss u card
Patterned Paper: Chatterbox, Inc.
Rub-ons: CI
Ribbons: May Arts, Offray & Son, Inc., MM

moments of solitude
Patterned Paper: The Rusty Pickle
Tag: The Rusty Pickle
Rub-ons: MM

nyc
Patterned Paper: MITM

pepsi
Cardstock: Bazzill
Patterned Paper: Chatterbox, Inc., DCWV
Tiles: JoAnn Essentials
Vellum Envelope: JoAnn Essentials
Jigsaw Letter: MM
Stickers: KI
Paint: MM

potty pride
Cardstock: Bazzill
Patterned Paper: The Paper Loft, 7 Gypsies
Stickers: JoAnn Essentials
Fabric Envelope: Li'l Davis Designs
Tag: JoAnn Essentials
Bubble: JoAnn Essentials
Safety Pin: MM
Ribbon: MM
Stamps: Ma Vinci's Reliquary
Ink: Ranger Industries
Fonts: Times New Roman, KM Funky Chicken

scooter girl
Cardstock: DCWV, Bazzill
Patterned Paper: Sassafras Lass
Stickers: Sassafras Lass
Tags: MM
Alphabet Conchos: Scrapworks, LLC
Chalk Ink: Clearsnap, Inc.
Font: Plastique, Serifa

the simple things
Patterned Paper: MITM
Stickers: MITM
3-D Embellishment: MITM

thoughts of bill
Patterned Paper: MM, Karen Foster Design
Vellum: JoAnn Fabric & Craft, Chatterbox, Inc.
Ribbon: My Mind's Eye, Inc.
Stickers: Chatterbox, Inc., Creative Memories
Ink: ColorBox
Paint: Delta Crafts
Font: 2 Peas Sleigh Ride

three boys
Cardstock: DCWV
Patterned Paper: DCWV
Stickers: DCWV
Overlay: DCWV
Tags: JoAnn Essentials
Brads: JoAnn Essentials
Metal Word: JoAnn Essentials
Metal Sticker: JoAnn Essentials
Floss: DMC

traditions at the pool
Patterned Paper: KI
Staples: MM
Brads: Doodlebug Designs Inc.
Stickers: CI
Mini Tags: MM
Acrylic Embellishment: Doodlebug Designs Inc.
Metallic Phrase: DCWV
Ribbon: FBTY

wild animals
Cardstock: DCWV
Patterned Paper: MITM
Tags: JoAnn Essentials
Eyelets: JoAnn Essentials

BUTTONS, BUBBLES & TILES

birthday wish pocket and tag
Card: MM
Patterned Paper: DCWV
Jelly Label: MM
Vellum Quote: JoAnn Essentials
Ribbon: MM
Beads: Blue Moon Beads
Gems: Blue Moon Beads

chill factor
Patterned Paper: CI
Stickers: CI

cuk
Cardstock: Chatterbox, Inc.
Patterned paper: Chatterbox, Inc.
Buttons: Junkitz
Stickers: Sonnets
Ribbon: Offray & Son, Inc.
Font: 2 Peas Flea Market

flower card
Patterned Paper: JoAnn Fabric & Crafts
Stickers: JoAnn Essentials
Button: MM
Ribbon: JoAnn Essentials, MM

freedom
Cardstock: Bazzill
Rub-ons: MM, Autumn Leaves
Brads: MM
Floss: MM
Bubbles: CI
Buttons: JoAnn Fabric & Crafts
Letters: JoAnn Fabric & Crafts

grandma's tackle box
Cardstock: Pebbles, Inc.
Patterned Paper: Sweetwater
Photo Turns: 7 Gypsies
Stickers: MAMBI
Rub-ons: CI
Metal Clips: 7 Gypsies
Negative Frames: CI
Ribbon: FBTY
Buttons: Chatterbox, Inc.
Bookplate: MM

heart breaker
Patterned Paper: SEI
Brads: SEI
Buttons: SEI
Ribbon: May Arts
Metal Letter: MM
Stickers: Sticker Studio, American Crafts
Stamps: PSX Design
Ink: Ranger Industries

holiday greetings card
Cardstock: DCWV
Patterned Paper: DCWV
Bubbles: JoAnn Essentials
Tiles: JoAnn Essentials
Brads: JoAnn Essentials
Fiber: JoAnn Essentials

home movies
Stickers: DCWV
Tiles: JoAnn Essentials
Gemstones: JoAnn Essentials
Overlay: DCWV
Stamps: Duncan Enterprises
Paint: Plaid Enterprises, Inc.
Font: 2 Peas Quirky

i love you card
Cardstock: DCWV
Patterned Paper: DCWV
Brads: JoAnn Essentials
Alphabet Buttons: JoAnn Essentials

ice cream fun
Cardstock: Bazzill
Patterned Paper: Scrappy Cat
Fiber: EK Success
Ribbon: Pine Cone Press
Brads: Magic Scraps
Tag: MM
Bookplate: MM
Alphabet Brads: JoAnn Essentials
Stickers: EK Success
Watch Crystal: Jest Charming

live it boy style
Patterned Paper: DCWV
Bookplate: JoAnn Essentials
Stickers: JoAnn Essentials, CI
Metal Letters: JoAnn Essentials
Bubbles: CI
Ink: Ranger Industries

mom mini album
Patterned Paper: DCWV
Tiles: JoAnn Essentials
Ribbon: Lifetime Moments
Flower: MM
Stamps: MoBe' Stamps, Image Tree
Paint: MM

nikki notepad
Patterned Paper: DCWV
Tiles: JoAnn Essentials
Candle: JoAnn Essentials
Rub-ons: Doodlebug Designs Inc.
Vellum Envelope: JoAnn Essentials

our european vacation
Cardstock: DCWV
Patterned Paper: DCWV
Bubbles: JoAnn Essentials
Tiles: JoAnn Essentials
Metallic Words: DCWV
Brads: JoAnn Essentials

recipe box
Cardstock: DCWV
Patterned Paper: DCWV
Bubbles: JoAnn Essentials
Buttons: JoAnn Essentials
Alphabet Brads: JoAnn Essentials
Metal Letters: JoAnn Essentials
Stickers: DCWV
Ribbon: DCWV

red, white, blue and you
Patterned Paper: MM, DCWV
Alphabet Buttons: JoAnn Essentials
Stencil Letters: JoAnn Essentials
Brads: JoAnn Essentials
Stamps: JoAnn Essentials
Bookplates: JoAnn Essentials
Tag: JoAnn Essentials
Metal Word: JoAnn Essentials
Metal Charm: JoAnn Essentials

scrapper's block jar
Canning Jar
Patterned Paper: Paperfever, Inc.
Tiles: JoAnn Essentials
Ribbon: Lifetime Moments

she's got a way about her
Cardstock: Bazzill
Patterned Paper: American Crafts, PC
Cardstock Quote: KI
Epoxy Word: Li'l Davis Designs
Epoxy Frames: Li'l Davis Designs
Leather Flower: MM
Photo Turns: MM
Brads: The Happy Hammer
Ink: ColorBox

slip-n-slide
Patterned Paper: KI
Stickers: Doodlebug Designs Inc.
Brad: JoAnn Essentials
Stamps: MM
Paint: Plaid Enterprises, Inc.

sunsets and sandcastles
Patterned Paper: BasicGrey
Stickers: Danielle Johnson
Brads: MM
Stamps: MM
Ink: Tsukineko
Font: 3 The Hardway

sweetie pie
Patterned Paper: Anna Griffin,
K & Company
Bubbles: JoAnn Essentials
Safety Pins: MM
Paper Flowers: MM
Ephemera: Melissa Frances
Stamps: MM
Paint: MM
Ink: Ranger Industries

swim
Patterned Paper: Marcella by Kay
Stickers: KI
Buttons: American Crafts
Brads: JoAnn Essentials
Tags: MM
Font: CK Toggle

**thinking of you
matchbook card**
Patterned Paper: KI
Button: Junkitz
Stamps: PSX Design
Ink: Tsukineko

you are
Cardstock: MM
Patterned Paper: CI, PC, Sonnets
Transparency: CI, Art Warehouse by
Danielle Johnson
Buttons: MM
Photo Corners: MM
Stickers: CI, MAMBI, Shotz by Danielle
Johnson
Stamps: MM
Ink: PSX Design

METALS

a late night swim
Patterned Paper: Scrapworks, LLC
Stickers: CI

Rub-ons: MM
Acrylic Sandals: Sarah Heidt Photo Craft
Metal Letters: MM
Brads: Scrappin' Extras
Buckle: Scrappin' Extras
Photo Hangers: Scrappin' Extras
Ribbon: Offray & Son, Inc.
Paint: MM
Font: CK Child

almost 4
Cardstock: DCWV, National Cardstock
Patterned Paper: SEI
Stamps: Diffusion Artistamps,
The Rusty Pickle
Eyelets: MM
Ink: CTMH, Ink It Up
Fonts: 2 Peas Flea Market

believe mini journal
Patterned Paper: DCWV
Bookplate: JoAnn Essentials
Brads: JoAnn Essentials
Mesh Fabric: JoAnn Fabric & Crafts
Believe Button: Dress It Up!

buds
Patterned Paper: MM
Stamps: MM
Bookplate: JoAnn Essentials
Conchos: Scrapworks, LLC

carnival
Cardstock: Bazzill
Patterned Paper: KI
Ribbon: Offray & Son, Inc., May Arts,
Wrights Ribbon Accents
Stamps: Ma Vinci's Reliquary, MM
Metal Hangers: Jest Charming
Embellishments
Ink: Stampin' Up

**celebrate card
and envelope**
Patterned Paper: Colorbok, Inc.
Frame: JoAnn Essentials
Vellum Quote: JoAnn Essentials
Fiber: JoAnn Essentials
Brads: JoAnn Essentials
Bookplate: JoAnn Essentials

cody & goofy
Cardstock: DCWV
Patterned Paper: DCWV
Brads: JoAnn Essentials
Metal Word: JoAnn Essentials
Word Charm: JoAnn Essentials
Eyelets: JoAnn Essentials
Bookplate: JoAnn Essentials
Stickers: Wordsworth Stamps, MAMBI,
Bo-Bunny Press
Rub-ons: Autumn Leaves

come out and play
Cardstock: Bazzill
Patterned Paper: BasicGrey
Rub-ons: MM
Wire: MM
Metal Moldings: MM
Paint: MM
Stickers: Pebbles, Inc., CI
Ink: Ranger Industries

confidence
Patterned Paper: Arctic Frog
Stickers: Pebbles, Inc., SEI
Stamps: The Rusty Pickle
Photo Corners: MM
Ribbon: May Arts
Rub-ons: Li'l Davis, Autumn Leaves, MM

create pocket journal
Patterned Paper: Colorbok, Inc.
Brads: JoAnn Essentials
Eyelets: JoAnn Essentials
Bookplates: JoAnn Essentials

Metal Charms: JoAnn Essentials
Word Brads: JoAnn Essentials
Vellum Envelopes: JoAnn Essentials

dreams
Cardstock: Bazzill
Patterned Paper: K & Company
Fibers: MM
Spiral Clips: MM
Word Charms: MM
Hinges: MM
Metal Numbers: MM
Metal Corners: MM
Acrylic Words: Doodlebug Designs Inc.
Eyelets: Doodlebug Designs Inc.
Ink: Ranger Industries

e i e i o
Cardstock: Bazzill
Patterned Paper:
Daisy D's Paper Company
Label Maker: Dymo
Ribbon: MM, MAMBI, Rebecca Sower,
Offray & Son, Inc.
Barcode Label: Mystic Press
Rub-ons: MM
Snaps: MM
Paper Flowers: MM
Eyelets: MM
Jump Rings: MM
Safety Pins: MM
Screw Eyelets: MM
Brads: MM
Clothespins: CI
Tags: Quickutz, American Tag Co..
Stamps: MM, HARS
Ink: Tsukineko
Paint: MM
Font: CK Constitution

electric
Cardstock: Bazzill
Patterned Paper: DCWV
Bookplates: JoAnn Essentials
Stickers: JoAnn Essentials, DCWV
Tag: JoAnn Essentials
Ribbon: Offray & Son, Inc., MM,
JoAnn Fabric & Crafts
Ink: Ranger Industries

family mini heritage album
Cardstock: DCWV
Patterned Paper: DCWV
Ribbon: DCWV
Alphabet Brads: JoAnn Essentials
Alphabet Conchos: JoAnn Essentials
Bookplate: JoAnn Essentials
Quote Stickers: DCWV
Stickers: DCWV
Tags: JoAnn Essentials
Metal Clips: MM

girlie girl
Cardstock: Bazzill
Patterned Paper: BasicGrey
Acrylic Stars: Paper Bliss
Brads: JoAnn Essentials, MM
Photo Turns: MM
Ribbon: Offray & Son, Inc.
Stickers: Chatterbox, Inc.
Font: Balzano

happy birthday card
Patterned Paper: DCWV
Bookplate: JoAnn Essentials
Brads: JoAnn Essentials
Vellum Quote: DCWV
Ribbon: Offray & Son, Inc.
Stamps: MM
Ink: Ranger Industries

inspirational journal
Journal: Paper Reflections
Patterned Paper: Colorbok, Inc., The Paper
Company
Heart Clip: JoAnn Essentials
Metal Plaque: JoAnn Essentials
Word Stick Pins: JoAnn Essentials

keaton bug
Cardstock: Bazzill
Patterned Paper:
Doodlebug Designs Inc.
Transparency Overlay: CI
Ribbon: Li'l Davis Designs,
Offray & Son, Inc.
Slide Mounts: Boxer Scrapbooks
Alphabet Squares: Junkitz
Brads: JoAnn Essentials
Tag Alphabet: MM
Metal Words: MM
Hinges: MM
Paint: Golden Artist Colors

love card and tag
Cardstock: Bazzill
Patterned Paper: 7 Gypsies
Metal Frame: DCWV
Rub-ons: MM
Jump-Rings: MM
Cardstock Tag: MM
Ribbon: MM
Paint: Plaid Enterprises, Inc.

magnetic calendar
Magnetic Canvas: Darice
Patterned Paper: Colorbok, Inc.
Bookplates: JoAnn Essentials
Ribbon: Offray & Son, Inc.

memories
Cardstock: DCWV
Patterned Paper: MITM
Word Charms: JoAnn Essentials
Metal Alphabet: JoAnn Essentials
Fiber: JoAnn Essentials
Metal Word: JoAnn Essentials

memories
Cardstock: Bazzill
Patterned Paper: 7 Gypsies
Photo Turns: 7 Gypsies
Letters: Foofala
Brads: The Happy Hammer
Ribbon: May Arts, Offray & Son, Inc.
Stamps: MM
Ink: Ranger Industries

memories box
Patterned Paper: DCWV
Metal Words: JoAnn Essentials
Bubble: JoAnn Essentials
Paint: Making Memories

memories of lois
Patterned Paper: Chatterbox, Inc.
Ribbon: Offray & Son, Inc.
Bookplate: JoAnn Essentials
Brads: JoAnn Essentials
Safety Pin: JoAnn Essentials
Rub-ons: MM

mom gift wrap and tag
Patterned Paper: DCWV
Tag: JoAnn Essentials
Metal Flower: JoAnn Essentials
Alphabet Stickers: JoAnn Essentials

my family
Cardstock: Bazzill
Patterned Paper: BasicGrey
Ribbon: May Arts
Stickers: American Crafts
Word Charms: JoAnn Essentials
Ink: Ranger Industries

my life at 16 journal
Cardstock: DCWV
Patterned Paper: MITM
Alphabet Tags: JoAnn Essentials
Metal Tag: JoAnn Essentials
Conchos: JoAnn Essentials
Stickers: DCWV

Bookplate: JoAnn Essentials
Bubbles: JoAnn Essentials
Brads: JoAnn Essentials

sisters
Patterned Paper: 7 Gypsies
Photo Turns: 7 Gypsies
Frame: 7 Gypsies
Index Tab: 7 Gypsies
Twill: 7 Gypsies
Ribbon: May Arts
Cardstock Tags: MM
Stamps: MM, Ma Vinci's Reliquary
Ink: Ranger Industries

smile
Cardstock: Bazzill
Patterned Paper: K & Company
Metal Strip: MM
Wood Letters: Li'l Davis Designs
Wood Frame: Li'l Davis Designs
Safety Pins: MM
Stamps: Wordsworth Stamps
Paint: MM

true friend
Cardstock: Bazzill
Patterned Paper: Chatterbox, Inc.
Punch: CI
Tag: JoAnn Essentials
Bookplate: JoAnn Essentials
Ribbon: Offray & Son, Inc.
Eyelets: MM
Metal Words: MM
Chalk: Stampin' Up
Vellum Quote: DCWV
Paint: American Accents
Stamps: MM
Ink: ColorBox

winter coaster magnet
Cardboard Coaster
Cardstock: DCWV
Patterned Paper: DCWV
Metal Charm: JoAnn Essentials
Word Eyelet: JoAnn Essentials
Letter Brad: JoAnn Essentials
Clear Buttons: 7 Gypsies
Fibers: FBTY
Silver Mesh: JoAnn Fabric & Crafts

wish upon a star
Cardstock: SEI
Patterned Paper: SEI
Brads: JoAnn Essentials
Bookplate: JoAnn Essentials
Word Charms: JoAnn Essentials
Stickers: SEI
Ribbon: SEI
Ink: Stampin' Up

wished for this
Cardstock: Bazzill
Patterned Paper: The Rusty Pickle
Brads: JoAnn Essentials
Conchos: JoAnn Essentials
Bookplate: JoAnn Essentials
Sticker: Doodlebug Designs Inc.
Acrylic Letters: Doodlebug Designs Inc.
Canvas Phrase: Li'l Davis Designs
Clay Phrase: Li'l Davis Designs
Cardstock Tag: MM
Safety Pin: MM
Leather Flowers: MM
Ribbon: Offray & Son, Inc., May Arts
Ink: Ranger Industries

you inspire me to be tag
Patterned Paper: DCWV
Metal Letters: JoAnn Essentials
Metal Word: JoAnn Essentials
Vellum Envelope: JoAnn Essentials
Fiber: FBTY
Ribbon: FBTY

3-D EMBELLISHMENTS

aloha card
Cardstock: DCWV
3-D Embellishments: JoAnn Essentials
Alphabet Buttons: JoAnn Essentials
Ink: ColorBox

beautiful flower girl
Cardstock: Bazzill
Patterned Paper: MITM
Vellum: MITM
Eyelet Tags: JoAnn Essentials
Metal Letters: JoAnn Essentials
3-D Embellishment: JoAnn Essentials
Tag: JoAnn Essentials
Vellum Quote: JoAnn Essentials
Fonts: Architect, Staccato222BT

create altered journal
Patterned Paper: DCWV
3-D Embellishments: JoAnn Essentials
Acrylic Embellishments: LazerLetterz
Fibers: FBTY
Ribbon: FBTY
Modge Podge: Plaid Enterprises, Inc.
Diamond Glaze: JudiKins
Stamps: HARS
Ink: Tsukineko

dad card
Cardstock: DCWV
Patterned Paper: DCWV
3-D Embellishments: JoAnn Essentials
Stamps: MoBe' Stamps

dad tin
3-D Embellishments: JoAnn Essentials
Ribbon: Lifetime Moments
Stamps: MoBe' Stamps
Paint: MM

engaged
Cardstock: DCWV
Patterned Paper: DCWV
3-D Embellishments: JoAnn Essentials
Stamps: MM
Ink: Tsukineko

first day
Cardstock: DCWV
Patterned Paper: DCWV
Stickers: DCWV
Tags: JoAnn Essentials
3-D Embellishments: JoAnn Essentials
Metal Sticker: JoAnn Essentials
Brads: JoAnn Essentials

first trip to the beach mini album
Cardstock: DCWV
Patterned Paper: DCWV
3-D Embellishments: JoAnn Essentials

flip-flop card
Cardstock: DCWV
Patterned Paper: The Paper Patch
3-D Embellishments: JoAnn Essentials
Stamp: Whipper Snapper Designs

flower card
Cardstock: DCWV
Patterned Paper: DCWV
3-D Embellishment: JoAnn Essentials

gratitude card
Cardstock: Bazzill
Brads: JoAnn Essentials
3-D Embellishment: JoAnn Essentials
Vellum Quote: JoAnn Essentials
Fonts: Bernie

i love my kitty accordion album
Accordion Album: DCWV
Cardstock: DCWV
Patterned Paper: DCWV
Overlay: DCWV
3-D Embellishment: JoAnn Essentials
Brads: JoAnn Essentials, The Happy Hammer
Tiles: JoAnn Essentials
Bookplates: JoAnn Essentials
Stickers: DCWV
Cork Embellishments: LazerLetterz
Fibers: FBTY
Stamps: Leave Memories
Ink: Ranger Industries, Stampin' Up

joy card
Sticker: DCWV
3-D Embellishments: JoAnn Essentials

joy tag
Tag: JoAnn Essentials
3-D Embellishment: JoAnn Essentials

majestic view
Cardstock: MITM
Patterned Paper: MITM
Brad: JoAnn Essentials
Tag: JoAnn Essentials
3-D Embellishments: JoAnn Essentials
Font: Raavi

my new family accordion frame
Accordion Album: DCWV
Patterned Paper: DCWV
3-D Embellishments: JoAnn Essentials
Ribbon: FBTY

one sweet world
Cardstock: DCWV, Bazzill
Patterned Paper: Scrapworks, LLC
Paper Flowers: JoAnn Fabric & Crafts
Ribbon: May Arts
Brads: K & Company, MM, Lasting Impressions
Metal Letters: MM
Sticker: Scrapworks, LLC
Rub-ons: Autumn Leaves, MM, Chatterbox, Inc.
Stamps: MM
Paint: DecoArt
Ink: Tsukineko

perfect summer day
Cardstock: DCWV
Patterned Paper: DCWV
Stickers: DCWV
Brads: JoAnn Essentials
Bookplate: JoAnn Essentials
Fiber: JoAnn Essentials
3-D Embellishments: JoAnn Essentials
Floss: DMC
Rickrack: Wrights Ribbon Accents
Ink: ColorBox

someday my prince will come
Patterned Paper: The Paper Loft, PSX Design
Fiber Paper: Magenta Rubber Stamps
Mesh: Magenta Rubber Stamps
Ribbon: Offray & Son, Inc.
Stickers: CI
Frame: Li'l Davis Designs
Ink: Colorbok, Inc.
Metal Letters: MM
Staples: MM
Stamps: Ma Vinci's Reliquary
Font: 2 Peas High Tide

the loveliest of all card
Cardstock: DCWV
Patterned Paper: The Paper Company
3-D Embellishments: JoAnn Essentials

tie card
Cardstock: DCWV
Patterned Paper: DCWV
3-D Embellishments: JoAnn Essentials

u are my sunshine
Cardstock: KI
Patterned Paper: KI
Tags: KI
Frames: KI
Brad: JoAnn Essentials
Fiber: JoAnn Essentials
Metal Embellishment: K & Company
Ribbon: May Arts
Jigsaw Puzzle: MM
Stickers: Doodlebug Designs Inc.
Rub-ons: MAMBI, Doodlebug Designs Inc.
Paint: MM
Ink: Ranger Industries

under construction
Patterned Paper: Karen Foster Design
Stickers: Karen Foster Design
Alphabet Brads: JoAnn Essentials
Ink: ColorBox

when my eyes meet your eyes
Cardstock: Bazzill
Patterned Paper: KI
Rub-ons: MM
Metal Letters: MM
Paper Flowers: MM
Metal Square: 7 Gypsies

where will they take you?
Patterned Paper: Chatterbox, Inc.
Die Cuts: MAMBI
Key: The Rusty Pickle
Stickers: EK Success, K & Company
Metal Word: MM
Metal Letter: MM
Fabric Word: MAMBI
Fonts: Pepita MT, Abadi MT

wishes card
3-D Embellishments: JoAnn Essentials
Tag: Sizzix
Ribbon: Offray & Son, Inc.
Stamp: Penny Black

ALPHABETS

a wish is a dream your heart makes
Patterned Paper: DMD Industries
Ribbon: Offray & Son, Inc.
Conchos: Scrapworks, LLC
Alphadotz: Scrapworks, LLC
Letters: Doodlebug Designs Inc., MM, EK Success, CI, Junkitz

art
Patterned Paper: Colorbok, Inc.
Screwhead Snaps: JoAnn Essentials
Bookplate: JoAnn Essentials
Clip Alphabet: JoAnn Essentials
Definition Bubbles: JoAnn Essentials
Brads: JoAnn Essentials
Sticker Alphabet: JoAnn Essentials

baby girl
Cardstock: DCWV
Patterned Paper: DCWV, MITM, BasicGrey
Stickers: DCWV
Concho Alphabet: JoAnn Essentials
Brads: JoAnn Essentials
Tag: JoAnn Essentials

Bookplate: JoAnn Essentials
Vellum Quote: JoAnn Essentials
Stamps: MM
Ink: Ranger Industries

big, blue eyes
Patterned Paper: DCWV
Scrabble Letters: DCWV
Stickers: DCWV
Metal Letters: JoAnn Essentials

candy door hanger
Cardstock: DCWV
Patterned Paper: DCWV
Alphabet Brads: JoAnn Essentials
Brads: JoAnn Essentials
Metal Charm: JoAnn Essentials
Ribbon: FBTY
Ink: Stampin' Up, Plaid Enterprises, Inc.

christmas advent calendar
Photo Flip Frame
Cardstock: DCWV
Patterned Paper: DCWV
Alphabet Brads: JoAnn Essentials
Tag: JoAnn Essentials
Alphabet Bubbles: JoAnn Essentials
Brads: JoAnn Essentials
Stickers: DCWV
Alphabet Stickers: JoAnn Essentials
Rub-ons: MM
Ribbon: Offray & Son, Inc.

exploring
Cardstock: DCWV
Patterned Paper: DCWV
Vellum Quote: DCWV
Alphabet Brads: JoAnn Essentials
Bookplate: JoAnn Essentials
Fiber: JoAnn Essentials
Staples: MM
Stamps: MM

he would rather be fishing
Patterned Paper: MITM
Laser Cuts: DCWV
Metal Letters: JoAnn Essentials
Vellum Quote: JoAnn Essentials
Tag: JoAnn Essentials
Hinges: MM
Fonts: CentSchbook BT, SF Remember, Milltown

john mayer concert
Cardstock: Bazzill, Chatterbox, Inc.
Patterned Paper: The Rusty Pickle
Brads: JoAnn Essentials
Bookplate: JoAnn Essentials
Stickers: Doodlebug Designs Inc., MM
Chipboard Letters: Li'l Davis Designs
Cardstock Tag: MM
Ribbon: May Arts
Rub-ons: Autumn Leaves
Ink: Ranger Industries

kaylee
Cardstock: Paperbilities
Patterned Paper: Club Scrap, Inc.
Alphabet Tags: JoAnn Essentials
Flower Eyelet: MM
Metal Clip: MM
Ink: ColorBox

kyle
Cardstock: Bazzill
Ribbon: Offray & Son, Inc.
Bookplates: JoAnn Essentials
Metal Letters: JoAnn Essentials
Safety Pin: MM
Stamps: HARS

laughter is a smile that burst
Patterned Paper: BasicGrey
Tag: BasicGrey
Rub-ons: MM, Li'l Davis Designs
Chipboard Alphabet: Li'l Davis Designs
Ribbon: May Arts
Font: Desyrel

love tag
Patterned Paper: DCWV
Metal Heart Clip: MM
Vellum Quote: JoAnn Essentials
Alphabet Brads: JoAnn Essentials
Brads: JoAnn Essentials
Stickers: DCWV

noel card
Cardstock: DCWV
Patterned Paper: DCWV
Alphabet Brads: JoAnn Essentials

our mini m & m's
Patterned Paper: CI
Stickers: JoAnn Essentials, CI, Chatterbox, Inc.
Ribbon: FBTY
Tags: MM
Stamps: PSX Design, MM

pumpkin picking
Cardstock: Bazzill
Stickers: MM
Alphabet Brads: JoAnn Essentials
Ribbon: Offray & Son, Inc.
Brads: Adorned Pages

rainy day fun
Cardstock: Bazzill
Crackle Medium: FolkArt
Metal Letters: JoAnn Essentials, Scrapworks, LLC, Pressed Petals
Acrylic Letter: Heidi Grace Designs
Bookplate: JoAnn Essentials
Mesh: MM
Tag: MM
Stamps: MM
Paint: MM

savor the moment
Cardstock: Bazzill, KI
Patterned Paper: Mustard Moon Paper Co., Chatterbox, Inc.
Ribbon: May Arts
Metal Letters: MM
Leather Flower: MM
Safety Pins: MM
Wood Letters: Li'l Davis Designs
Icicle Letters: KI
Hardware: 7 Gypsies
Stamps: MM, PSX Design
Ink: Ranger Industries
Font: 2 Peas Mister Giggles

sisters and friends
Cardstock: Bazzill
Patterned Paper: KI
Quotes: KI
Ribbon: May Arts
Alphabet Tag: JoAnn Essentials
Metal Word: JoAnn Essentials
Stickers: KI
Ink: ColorBox

snyders
Cardstock: DCWV
Patterned Paper: DCWV
Metal Letters: JoAnn Essentials
Metal Word Eyelets: JoAnn Essentials
Metal Charms: JoAnn Essentials
Fibers: JoAnn Essentials
Brads: JoAnn Essentials
Stamps: PSX Design
Ink: Tsukineko

so happy together card
Library Pocket: Autumn Leaves
Patterned Paper: SEI
Ribbon: SEI, MM, Jest Charming
Tags: SEI, MM
Rub-ons: SEI, MM
Ink: Ranger Industries
Flower Brad: MM
Metal Charms: MM
Page Pebble: MM
Staples: MM
Bottle Cap Alphabet: Li'l Davis Designs
Alpha Tokens: Doodlebug Designs Inc., Junkitz
Foo-fa-bet: Foofala
Font: P22 Garamouche, Autumn Leaves Cadence

timeless
Cardstock: Bazzill
Patterned Paper: The Rusty Pickle
Clock Hand: Walnut Hollow
Key: Magic Scraps
Metal Letters: MM
Ribbon: MM
Stamps: HARS
Paint: MM

too sexy for my hair
Cardstock: Bazzill
Patterned Paper: Scenic Route Paper Co., Colorbok, Inc.
Metal Alphabet Charms: JoAnn Essentials, MM
Stickers: EK Success, Dymo
Brads: MM
Metal Hinges: MM
Playing Cards: 7 Gypsies
Corner Punch: EK Success
Ink: Stampin' Up

travel
Cardstock: DCWV
Patterned Paper: DCWV
Alphabet Brads: JoAnn Essentials
Vellum Quote: JoAnn Essentials
Bubbles: JoAnn Essentials
Vellum Envelope: JoAnn Essentials
Tag: JoAnn Essentials
Fiber: JoAnn Essentials

tristan
Patterned Paper: BasicGrey
Tags: BasicGrey
Concho: Scrapworks, LLC
Stickers: Sonnets, BasicGrey, Hot Off The Press, CI, Wordsworth Stamps
Heart Eyelet: MM
Brads: JoAnn Essentials
Ribbon: MM

what could be better...
Cardstock: Bazzill
Patterned Paper: Daisy D's Paper Company
Bookplate: MM
Tags: MM
Brads: MM
Ribbon: May Arts
Stickers: American Crafts, Sticker Studio
Ink: Ranger Industries

winter wish card
Patterned Paper: DCWV
Letters: JoAnn Essentials
Metal Charms: JoAnn Essentials
Word Charm: JoAnn Essentials
Brads: JoAnn Essentials

your smile
Patterned Paper: CI
Stickers: CI

About the Author

Nancy M. Hill began designing scrapbook pages nearly 35 years ago, and wishes she could retire and scrapbook full-time. Before founding DieCuts With a View and The Scrapbook Institute, she was a college professor and administrator with a Ph. D in business and information systems. She has consulted both nationally and internationally in the corporate and private sector as a marketing and institutional researcher and strategic planner. She is a Board Certified Genealogist and prolific writer with more than 200 publications to her credit. She and her husband, Mike, are fortunate to live close to and work professionally with their nine children and seven grandchildren.